HAVING, GIVING, HOPING

Having, Giving, Hoping

Leonardo Polo

Translated by
Roderrick Esclanda
Alberto I. Avargas

Leonardo Polo Institute of Philosophy Press
2023

Spanish Original
Copyright © 2015 Fundación Studium

English Translation
Copyright © 2023 The Leonardo Polo Institute of Philosophy

All rights reserved. This book or any portion thereof may not be reproduced or used in any manner whatsoever without the express written permission of the publisher except for the use of brief quotations in a book review or scholarly journal.

ISBN 978-0-9912568-5-3

Cover image:
Vincent van Gogh, *Terrace and Observation Deck at the Moulin de Blute-Fin, Montmartre*, early 1887
Art Institute of Chicago

Leonardo Polo Institute of Philosophy
1121 North Notre Dame Ave.
South Bend, IN 46617

www.leonardopoloinstitute.org

Table of Contents

Introduction vii
   Greek anthropology: man as the being capable of having ... viii
      Having viii
      The first level of having: corporeal and practical having ... x
      The second level of having: immanent possession xiii
      The third level of having: habits xv
      Summary of Polo's anthropology of having xvii
   The Christian Perspective on the Human Person xviii
      The will and gifting xviii
      Destining and hope xx
      Hope and the future xxi

Having, Giving, Hoping 1
   1. Having: Notes Concerning Greek Anthropology 2
      1.1 Man facing the universe: from classical to modern
      anthropology 2
      1.2 The Greek definition of man: the animal that has 5
      1.3 Practical having: means and ends 10
      1.4 Immanent possession: theory and practice 20
      1.5 Habits: growth and cybernetics 28
      1.6 Knowledge and virtue as the culmination of life 30
   2. Giving: Notes on Christian Anthropology 39
      2.1 Desiring and loving: "operosity" of love and
      hyperteleology 39
      2.2 The person: giving as loving bestowal 45
      2.3 Free destining 46
      2.4 Intimacy 50
      2.5 Reason's offering and faith 52
   3. Hoping 54
      3.1 Optimism 54
      3.2 The future and the task 57

3.3 Risk 58
3.4 Convoking help 60
3.5 Revolutionaries and terrorists 61
3.6 Voluntarism and nihilism in modern philosophy ... 64
3.7 The nothingness of the other as love of self 67
3.8 The hopeful task 69
3.9 Business and hope 71

Books by Leonardo Polo *75*

Introduction

Having, Giving, Hoping is a short work by Leonardo Polo in which he presents the basic outlines of a philosophical anthropology that gathers together insights from classical Greek philosophy (especially Aristotle), Christian anthropology, and modern thought.

The present text is based on a three-day seminar given to business people at the PAD Business School in Lima (Peru) in July 1984[1], and also draws from two other conferences given in Bogota (Colombia) that same year[2]. These articles were then revised and expanded with a section on Christian anthropology and hope, and published as "Tener, dar y esperar" in a new volume of Polo's writings titled *Filosofía y economía*[3], which would then be published under the same title as part of Leonardo Polo's *Complete Works*[4].

The tone and style of this work fit the audience and context for whom it was first presented: business executives at seminars and conferences at business schools in Latin America. As such, Polo offers an overview of a philosophical

---

[1] First published in 1987: Leonardo Polo, "Tener y dar" in F. Fernández (ed.), *Estudios sobre la encíclica 'Laborem exercens'*, BAC, Madrid 1987, pp. 201-230. Then published again as Leonardo Polo, *Sobre la existencia cristiana*, Eunsa, Madrid 1996, chapter 2. Starting with it's 2nd edition, the title of this book was changed to *Sobre la originalidad de la concepción cristiana de la existencia*, Eunsa, Pamplona 2010. It is currently published as part of Polo's Complete Works: *Obras completas de Leonardo Polo*, v. XIII, Eunsa, Pamplona 2015, pp. 227-253.

[2] Eventually published as "Tres dimensiones de la antropología" in *Studia Poliana*, Pamplona, 13 (2011), 15-29.

[3] Leonardo Polo, *Filosofía y economía*, Eunsa, Pamplona 2012.

[4] Leonardo Polo, *Filosofía y economía* (*Obras completas de Leonardo Polo*, v. XXV), Eunsa, Pamplona 2015, pp. 193-256.

anthropology that seeks to frame human productive and economic activity within a wider vision of the dynamism of the human person, done in a clear and simple manner that avoids technical jargon, but at the same time remains deeply philosophical.

Polo begins "Having, Giving, Hoping" with the observation that the systematic study of the human being can be undertaken from three different perspectives:

> The *static* or *constitutive* aspects of the human being (human nature, composition, etc.);

> The human being in her *dynamism*, which includes the study of human operations and actions;

> The human being from the perspective of existential questions that arise from how the human person is constituted, and therefore as a problematic or *tragic* being.

In his essay, Polo considers these three aspects as they appear in history, starting with the Greek understanding of man as the being capable of having, followed by the Christian vision of person as gift, and finally the modern and contemporary attitude regarding human existence, which is tragic.

Greek anthropology: man as the being capable of having

Having

Polo begins his study of the human being with Greek anthropology, which asks: *what* is man? This anthropology seeks to define man by looking at human nature so as to identify how it differs from any other nature; in other words, the Greeks seek to understand what man's distinctive characteristic is.

Introduction

This Greek definition of man can be found in Aristotle, and it is often said that for Aristotle, man is a rational animal. In this reading, what man has in common with other animals is, precisely, that he is an animal, with a body and with sensible life. On the other hand, what is peculiar, or unique, about man is rationality.

While Polo accepts that rationality is, indeed, a characteristic that differentiates man from other animals, he nevertheless believes that Aristotle points to a deeper defining characterization of man: namely, that man is capable of *having*. Here, Polo offers a reading of Aristotle that differs from the more widely accepted (and sometimes formulaic) standard presentation of Aristotle's thought, and instead proposes an interpretative key that he considers to be more in tune with the deeper core inspirations of Aristotle's philosophical anthropology. In this regard, Polo points out that Aristotle defines man not so much as a rational animal, but rather as an animal that *has* reason (*logos*), and, in Polo's view, a number of Aristotle's texts show that it is *having* that distinguishes man from all other beings: having reason, having some kind of characteristic, having things, etc. Man is thus "the being that, different from the others, maintains a relation of having with his constitutive properties and with the rest of the world." Thus, for example, to be rational is (in Polo's reading of Aristotle) "to be capable of possessing everything in the form of an idea or of an object upon knowing it." In this way, Polo expresses that being capable of having is more fundamental than being rational; in fact, man is rational insofar as he *has* reason.

Polo then observes that for the Greeks, man is capable of maintaining several different levels of relationships of appropriation; in other words, man's relationship of having can be more or less intense, depending on which dimensions of his nature is involved.

These different intensities form three different levels of having:

Having according to man's body and his productive capability (the corporeal-practical level);

Having according to what is rational in man (the level of immanent operation);

Having in man's very nature as an acquired perfection or habit (the level of intrinsic perfection of human nature).

Aside from there being different levels of having, these levels are, according to Polo, hierarchically ordered among themselves. This means that some levels are subordinate to other higher ones in such a way the lower forms of having are ordered to the higher ones as means to ends. The superior levels, on the other hand, act as ends for the inferior levels.

In the context of Polo's philosophical anthropology this hierarchical relationship of the different levels of having is key to being able to situate economic and business activity within the broader picture of human action, which, in turn, would be of great use to business people, who are the intended audience of this essay. Thus, for example, work and productive-economic activity, which involves man's corporeal-practical action (the first level of having), is subordinated to and is a means for immanent rational operations (the second level of having). These immanent operations are, in turn, subordinated to and are a means toward virtues, which perfect human nature in a stable way (the third level of having).

From this perspective, then, economic and business activities are placed within a broader context of human existing that involves operations of the spiritual faculties of the human person and the acquisition of virtues by which the human being grows in their capacity to do good.

The first level of having: corporeal and practical having

The first level of having involves corporeal and practical having. This level of having stems from a central observation that Polo makes about human beings: in contrast with other animals whose bodies are adapted to and specialized for survival in their specific environment, the bodies of human beings are open, and insofar as this entails being able to have, a human being is unique among animals in that she can possess with her body. Thus, for a human being, dressing or putting on clothes involves *having* clothes. Animals, on the other hand, do not possess with their bodies; they never really *have* clothing. An animal may be covered with fur, but its skin or fur is not something distinct from its body that they take and *have*—they are simply a part of the animal's body, not possessions of their bodies.

One important continuation of this corporeal having things is *practical activity* by which human beings make instruments and relate them to each other in instrumental plexuses, which then together form the world that humans inhabit. Here, Polo makes reference to Thomas Aquinas, who notes that other animals aside from man have by nature what they need to survive and grow: claws by which they can defend themselves, or fur to keep them warm, for example. The human being, on the other hand, seems to be lacking in what she needs to survive. Aquinas, however, does not see this as true, because, he argues, nature *has* provided each human being with *hands* and *reason* by which she can make what she needs: with hands and reason, the human being can have in such a way that she has instruments that can be used and thus she can make what she needs. For example, a human being can take a hammer with her hands and use it as an instrument to hammer nails, which then makes it possible for her to build shelter or weapons needed for her survival; or she can take a musical instrument through which she plays a melody.

The crucial element here is not just that human beings have reason, but that they have hands: Polo points out that a hand does not terminate in itself, but rather communicates its dynamism to what is at hand. Thus, with hands, human beings can intervene in the material world through practical action and they can thereby take external things and make them into tools, which then come to form part of that practical activity. Within this set of practical activities, each one of the things that is had by the human being refers to other things; that is, a set of references exists between each of these things because they are all had. In this way, they thereby constitute a plexus of signifying or medial references, which forms the habitat that human beings inhabit:

"A set of references exists between these things precisely because they are all had. I have the hammer in the hand; with the hammer, I make reference to the nail; the hammer itself is ordered to the nail. The nail is for nailing; nailing is for making the table; the table is also for using. In this way, a plexus of medial references is constituted."

From this perspective, "the inhabitable world is the plexus of medial references":

"We articulate the world because we communicate our having it to it. Things co-belong to each other in our world. There is a relationship between this table and this tray; between this tray and this glass; between the pitcher and the water. All this constitutes a plexus of signifying references that are the inhabitable world."

The world that is thus constituted by human beings' practical activity is a common world: it is a plexus that is constructed and understood by many persons, and therefore exists not just for one person, but for the community. Consequently, while it is true that man is naturally entitled to ascribe a part of this plexus to himself as private property, this right is not absolute in the sense that it cannot be completely separated from the medial plexus as a whole. The plexus can therefore be said to be public and private at the same time.

Polo applies his understanding of the world of practical activity as a web of instrumental plexuses to related areas of study in other works. In *Rich and Poor*, for example, Polo expands his analysis to broader economic and organizational questions, and contrasts his findings with both Marxism and 20th-century economic liberalism. One central point that Polo insists on is that business and economic activity should be based not only on demand, but above all on supply, and that this view arises from an understanding of the richness of the human person. In the context of this present work, however, these considerations involve, first of all, an inquiry into the other levels of having.

The second level of having: immanent possession

Although corporeal-practical having and the capability of organizing an instrumental plexus is one way that distinguishes man from other animals, it is neither the only nor the highest level of having. After his discussion of corporeal-practical having, Polo turns his attention to the next level of having: that *of immanent operations* of the intellect:

"In Plato, as well as in Aristotle, there is the very deep conviction that the level of corporeal-practical having, while very important and peculiar to man, is, nevertheless, not the highest. Above this possession are the so-called immanent operations."

Polo contrasts *immanent operations* with the practical activities of the first level of having, which often entail making or producing things. In these "making" activities, the activity is directed towards an end. This end is a product that results in something external to the activity. This product acts as the *end* or *goal* of the practical activity, and once this end is achieved, the activity ceases. The *action of building*, for example, is an activity whose end is a building, and the activity continues as long as the building is not yet completed; once completed, however, the activity of building ceases. By *immanent operation*, on the other hand, Polo means "that human activity according to which man possesses a thing that (upon being possessed) does not remain external, but instead is intrinsic to the possessive operation." Unlike the activity of making things, immanent operations are not activities that terminate outside the activity itself. Instead, immanent operations possess their ends in the activity itself, and are thus called *perfect operations*. In perfect operations, the end is *already* possessed with the operation, unlike making in which the activity continues until the end is achieved, and once this end is achieved, the practical activity ends. For example, with the immanent action of seeing, I *already* possess what I see *as* I am seeing. There is no seeing that is striving to attain what is seen; instead, I see what I see *as* I see, and what I see is intrinsically possessed by the operation of seeing.

Another example of an immanent operation is thinking: through the operation of thinking, man possesses that which is thought in the very operation of thinking; that is, as maintained in the operation itself. Thus, I have that which is thought inasmuch as I think it. This last example is of particular relevance here because it is by the immanent operations of the intellect that man is called a "rational animal", since to be rational is to possess intimately.

An immanent operation is a form of possession that is more intimate and higher than corporeal-practical having. The corporeal-practical level of having (of the instrumental plexus) is therefore related to this second level of having (of immanent possession) as means are to an end; immanent operations are, in turn, ends for corporeal-practical having, and it is immanent operations that make corporeal-practical having possible (production presupposes theory). The immanent operations of reason are a condition for understanding the practical plexus and for acting within it. Thus, while practical activity is important, it must be kept in mind that it is only a means, and that its end is progress in the acquisition of truth (as acquired by the immanent operations of the intellect). This also means that the practical activity arises from thought and is organized by thought such that the instrumental plexus that configures the economic activity of the world relies on a culture of knowledge, and education[5].

---

[5] See, for example "El saber humano y la historia: el tema del destino y la libertad" (*Obras completas de Leonardo Polo*, v. XVIII, Eunsa, Pamplona 2019, pp. 23-60) and "Historia y libertad" (*Obras completas de Leonardo Polo*, v. XVIII, Eunsa, Pamplona 2019, pp. 61-86).

The third level of having: habits

After studying corporeal-practical having and immanent possession through immanent operations, Polo brings his attention to bear on the third level of having: that of *habits*.

Polo's understanding of habits stems from a cybernetic interpretation of immanent operations. By this, he means that the exercise of immanent operations gives rise to a sort of feedback in the principle of these acts; that is, the exercise of immanent operations modifies the structure of the faculty in a stable way, either perfecting it or making it worse:

"If an operation is exercised, feedback is produced: the structure of the faculty is modified, and the next act is better or worse."

This modification of a faculty as a consequence of the exercise of its acts is generally called a *habit*. If it perfects the faculty, it is called a *virtue*, while the imperfection that is a consequence of a defective exercise of its acts is called a *vice*. Virtues are called *intellectual* if they perfect the intellect or *moral* if they perfect the tendencies.

Insofar as virtues are stable perfections of man's intellect and will, they intrinsically perfect human essence:

"Virtue is a stable disposition: it becomes incorporated into the being of the one who has it. For this reason, it is said that it is a 'second nature'."

Virtue can therefore be called a *hyperformalization* of the human being's spiritual faculties (her intellect and will). This hyperformalization means that, with virtue, the human being is capable of operations that she was not previously capable of and, by exercising higher operations, she is capable of an increase in virtue. By growing in virtue then, the faculties become ever more perfect, making possible ever higher operations and virtues:

"And from this modification, a new form of activity follows. There is an operative gain of virtue: acts engender virtues, and virtues make new acts possible."

This hyperformalization thus broadens the scope of what is possible: it makes possible that which was not possible in a previous state. Polo explains that, for example, it might not be immediately possible to reach C from A; but insofar as A makes B possible, and B makes C possible, C does become possible from A, but by passing through intermediate states:

"For this reason, human life is not a serial process, as, for example, positivists understand it: if A, then B; if B, then C. That is, from A, B and C follow successively. In man's case, insofar as he is a hyperformal functional system, this is not the case; rather, A makes B possible, and B makes C possible; but it cannot be said that A makes C possible, because only the formal increase achieved from B opens up the possibility of C. There is a situation C that is impossible from situation A and, yet, not completely impossible."

This observation is important when it comes to the calculation or forecasting of objectives starting from any given situation: "What is foreseen as feasible from some starting point is ordinarily not much, because as long as a new point of departure has not been attained, the horizon of possibilities is narrow. This renewal of initiative—from what is initial—is what is characteristic of hyperformalization. While taking into account the available resources, calculation presents certain projects as possible; and it also states that the increase of resources would allow other more ambitious projects to be undertaken. Calculation, however, counts on what is given; hyperformalization is something else: it is not an increase of resources, but innovation in the principle of the acts."

So, just as Polo's recognition of immanent operations (the second level of having) frames practical and economic activity within a wider perspective, his acknowledgment of habit as a third level of having that perfects human faculties also adds a new dimension to our understanding of economics. Consequences of interest to businesses include, for example: (a) economic activity is not just a zero-sum game; (b) business decisions and strategy are based not only on calculations done from static starting points; (c) habits as perfections that make possible new operations mean that practical activity can grow with ever new possibilities and horizons.

Summary of Polo's anthropology of having

At the end of this first section of his essay, Polo summarizes the main points achieved by Greek anthropology.

First, man is distinguished from other animals by his capacity to have:

"Greek anthropology, in its most mature form, defines man by establishing his differential character: man is the being that can have."

Second, the human person has in different ways: corporeal-practical having, immanent having through cognitive operations, having as virtue.

Third, these different ways of having are hierarchically ordered in such a way that an inferior level depends on a superior one; this dependency is expressed according to a "means-ends" relationship—that is, the inferior level serves as a means with respect to the superior level. Thus, just as corporeal-practical having is a means with respect to immanent operations, immanent operations are, in turn, means for habits. In other words, immanent operations are ordered to virtues, and it is virtue that really perfects man.

At this point, Polo considers his survey of Greek anthropology finished, and he now moves on to consider what the Christian view of the human person adds to the consideration of philosophical anthropology.

The Christian Perspective on the Human Person

The will and gifting

Having covered the classical, Aristotelian perspective concerning man, Polo now looks to the Christian perspective concerning the human person. According to Polo, one aspect of the human person that Aristotle did not completely develop was that the will too is capable of perfect (or teleological) operations. For Polo, this is also where the Christian perspective enters.

Polo points out that for the Greeks, cognitive operations are perfect acts: they are acts that *already* possess their objects or ends simultaneously with the exercise of the operation itself. For example, if one thinks, then one *already* possesses what is thought. The will, on the other hand, is seen by the Greeks as not possessive:

"Neither in Aristotle nor in Plato (nor in any Greek thinker) is the will possessive; it is tendential, or rather, more precisely, non-possessive."

Instead of being possessive, the will's actions entail a *tending* to its object, to the good, but not a complete possession of that end or good. Thus, the will is always, at least according to classical philosophy, imperfect. A consequence of this (again from the pagan point of view) is that the will, insofar as it is understood only as tendency and desire (and therefore as imperfect), cannot be found in God. For the Christian, however, God is pure act, and, although He is Love, this Love excludes the potentiality and imperfection that desire in classical philosophy entails.

Furthermore, in Christianity, the will is a divine attribute, and this means that the will is regarded not just as a desire for something that it lacks, but as a perfection. Christianity thus brings with it a sense of the will that goes beyond the Greek notion of desire or tendency; it brings with it an understanding of God's love as a perfect act. This Christian discovery of love as perfect act (in contrast to desire, which is always imperfect) has repercussions in anthropology. More specifically, the will in man is no longer only desire:

"Christianity opens up perspectives that had been until then obscured or inaccessible. The only thing noble in man was his disinterested activity, that is, theory. The activities of the will were not disinterested; instead, they were tendential. And they remained either in the realm of useful tendencies or were directed towards knowledge."

Christian anthropology thus views the will in man not just as a desiring or a tendency to an end (*telos*), but, beyond this, as a *gifting* or as a *giving* without loss. Instead of a desire or longing (*eros*) that seeks to arrive at an end, gifting is an overflowing love that bestows, that gives, it is a giving that gives without losing. The human person is therefore not limited to being a being that is capable of having. Beyond having, or, more precisely, more deeply than having, the human person is capable of giving. This points to a principle within the person that goes more deeply than immanence and even virtue. This principle of gifting is what Polo calls "person"[6] or "intimacy".

For Polo, the person is origin of acts and is beyond having: with her *intimacy*, she not only *has*, but she also *gifts*. The opening up of personal intimacy brings with it the appearance in the world of novelties; the human person is not limited to initiating actions, but rather *adds*: the person adds acts that never before existed in the world, the person adds to the world by bestowing operatively. The human person is thus an "innovating being" and she is so because she *contributes* to the world from within herself. As a being that gives of herself, the human person proposes for herself goals that are higher than what is allowed by the means-end or the tendency-objective relationship (actions described as teleological, which are directed to an end (*telos*)).

---

[6] For a more extensive presentation of Polo's philosophical proposal and of his notion of person, see Leonardo Polo, *Why a Transcendental Anthropology?*, Leonardo Polo Institute of Philosophy Press, South Bend 2015, pp. 96 ff. Translated by Greg Chafuen, Roderrick Esclanda and Alberto I. Vargas.

Thus, if, for the Greeks, man is distinguished or defined by his capability for having, the Christian perspective views the person as a being that *is additionally* to the world. This does not deny the Greek view, but rather transcends it: man's possessive capability is, ultimately, sanctioned and ratified by a deeper instance, which is the person; *having* is continued and endorsed in the form of *gifting*:

"Consequently, the Greek definition of man is not denied; something is added to it that does not form part of that definition, but rather transcends and sustains it. Man's possessive capacity is, ultimately, sanctioned, ratified; but it is, moreover, sustained by a strictly radical instance that keeps it from being detained in possession, from ending in itself: it is projected or opens up, so to speak, as a vector of transcendence."

Destining and hope

Since gifting involves loving bestowal, it also implies a *destining* of action to someone who accepts it (or, in other words, a *beneficiary* of the destining action). Furthermore, if in Greek thought the terminus of desire is the possession of an end that was desired, here, in the Christian perspective, the terminus of destining is a terminus of offering. This means that our actions go beyond simply achieving a goal; they are, instead *destined* to someone who will accept them:

"The structure of love insofar as it is a perfect act implies a response: someone who is at the same level as the gifting."

In other words, if offering/gift-love is to be considered superior to simply desiring, it requires that there be *another person* who *accepts* my offering, who is the *beneficiary* of my actions and who *accepts* my offering. Without this other person, my offering cannot truly become a gift.

This new dimension of gift, which was absent from the Greek conception of man as a being capable of having, implies a new sense of *hope*, one that is based on loving reciprocity. Hope is therefore not a tendency to an end (as desire is); but rather a love that seeks correspondence. Hope is the search for acceptance and for response; it is a hope for finding a likeness. A likeness in this sense who is not merely a copy or a reiteration, but rather an alterity of initiatives in replica. If I am to be capable of loving in this way, the other has to be in such a way that she is not inferior to me, nor deprived of the capability to correspond to my love.

Hope and the future

Another dimension of hope in Polo is that it is not homeostatic, it does not seek to maintain an equilibrium; it is, instead, always dissatisfied, and refuses to settle down. This dissatisfaction is distinct from the dissatisfaction of the Greek *oretic* will, which is a dissatisfaction of hunger for an end that it longs for and desires. The dissatisfaction of hope, on the other hand, is a not being satisfied with the current situation because one aspires for more: it is a dissatisfaction of hope-filled *optimism*:

"The optimism of the man who lives in hope is dissatisfied because he is never reduced to the present."

The person who lives in hope affirms that we are in a world that can be improved, which is why she does not settle down comfortably in the present, but rather lives or exists precisely within the trajectory that leads to what is better. This means that hope is formed from an optimism that refers to the *future*. It includes putting oneself to the test: leaving the present situation in search of another.

Polo contrasts his understanding of hope with the Leibnizian idea that this is the best of all possible worlds, which would imply that there is nothing left to do, nothing that man can contribute to the world, and therefore a world without hope. In contrast to this, the person who lives in hope seeks to better the world through human actions that *add* to the world. Hope is therefore dissatisfied with the present world, not because it perceives the world as evil, but because it seeks something better.

In this way, Polo views the future as a *task* that entails a commitment, and therefore as a duty. This task also involves *risk*, and risk draws our attention to the *generosity of love*. Why would someone take a risk? Polo's answer is that she does so because she *accepts giving* under insufficient conditions. As such, this task is a dimension of hope inasmuch as *hope is the unfolding of the person's gift capacity*: the person's task is to *offer and contribute*, and she does this with *novelties that involve risk*.

All these considerations manifest themselves in Polo's understanding of business and of the businessperson, and they can be said to form a sort of gift game theory[7]. According to Polo, a businessperson is someone who exists in hope. As such, a business is a hope-filled task and thus entails not just meeting a need or a demand of the market, but also involves innovative, creative giving. Furthermore, someone involved in business is often faced with insufficient resources that prevents them from being able to do it all by themselves and keeps them from being able to handle the risk involved. A businessperson, however, treats this as an opportunity to convoke others for a task that is taken up for others and is fruitful. The businessperson is thus no longer a passive spectator or a passive pessimist; instead, she is someone who freely accepts her calling and contributes to the betterment of this world through tasks that bring something new and innovative to the world.

Roderrick Esclanda and Alberto I. Vargas
Chicago, Illinois
February 11, 2023

---

[7] See Gonzalo Alonso-Bastarreche and Alberto I. Vargas, "Gift Game Metatheory: Social Interaction and Interpersonal Growth" in *Frontiers in Psychology* (Vol. 12 - September 7, 2021), Article 687617; https://doi.org/10.3389/fpsyg.2021.687617

Having, Giving, Hoping

Leonardo Polo

I will attempt a comprehensive presentation of anthropology. The exposition can follow two criteria. First, a historical criterion. If one begins with the great Greek philosophers (the first ones to deal with psychology, ethics and politics or, more broadly, with what concerns human nature), one then has to move on to Christian thought (because, at least from the point of view of Western culture, it quickly comes up), in order to, lastly, deal with modern anthropology.

Another way of framing anthropology is systematic. This approach can, in turn, continue along three main directions, depending on how it deals with the different dimensions of man. I call the first *constitutional anthropology*, since it speaks of how man is, of what he is composed of, what his nature is, etc., and considers these factors from the, so to speak, static point of view.

I will call the second direction of systematic anthropology *dynamic anthropology*; that is, the study of human operating. Included here are history, sociology, the theory of technology and of culture, etc. This focus is constant (through the different epochs), but has perhaps been emphasized more in the 19th and 20th centuries.

It is possible, furthermore, to approach anthropology as a system of notions, from the strictly problematic point of view; that is, by focusing on man as a problem. I will call this direction *tragic anthropology*; it is the inquiry into the meaning of life. Man is effectively made (or constructed) in a specific way. But why is he made like this? Man acts; but in the end, for what reason does he act? Does the human phenomenon have meaning, or are we a useless passion?

There can be no doubt that it is very important to know what man is; and also to know of what nature his action is. But on man's horizon, a very specific question always appears, which, even though at times there is an attempt to cover it up, implicitly or latently remains: How will this end? Will it end well or badly? Is the outcome of what is human positive or is it not? This is what was earlier called tragic anthropology, and which, in the Christian perspective, could be better called dramatic, since the tragic belongs more properly to ancient times. Some of these tragic or dramatic elements of anthropology (today abundantly studied) include, for example, the sense of terror in the face of catastrophes that threaten us: nuclear war, ecological imbalance, etc.

Thus, three directions within the systematic approach are possible: constitutional anthropology, dynamic anthropology, and tragic anthropology. These three ways of dealing with the theme of man appear in all epochs: in Greek philosophers, as well as in Christian humanism, and in modern formulations. Sometimes the constitutional approach predominates; at other times, the dynamic one, etc. But in none of the historical epochs of anthropology is this triple approach neglected.

1. Having: Notes Concerning Greek Anthropology

1.1 Man facing the universe: from classical to modern anthropology

If we follow the double criteria mentioned—historical and systematic—then we must first of all study how the great Greek humanists understood man. This is not due to a mere erudite interest: it is strictly relevant today, because Greek thought has decisively influenced subsequent anthropology. Moreover, this anthropology contains fundamental insights, even though they are not complete, since within it a number of important human themes are not formulated well or even pass unperceived; for example, the theme of the person, which is not pagan but Christian. The Greeks understood that man is a nature: but they really did not come to see what personal being is. Another one of these themes that is poorly dealt with or without an adequate solution concerns evil, which in turn opens up another way of considering human-drama[1]. Nevertheless, apart from these limitations, the work of the great Greek thinkers, through their great insights in their understanding of man, represents a contribution that cannot be ignored.

In order to understand the nucleus of Greek anthropology in a condensed way, it can be said that it refers to what man is; it deals above all with the question of his nature insofar as this nature is different from any other[2]. The Greeks sought out man's distinctive character. To investigate a reality from the differential point of view is to seek its definition, since the procedure for achieving this is precisely to define it: to establish the characteristics that this reality has in common with others and, at the same time, what in it is specific; its difference is thereby established. This is the first thing that the Greeks did: seek out that which is irreducible in man with respect to any other observable entity. The definition they found is precise and clear, even though the complexity of the task can at times become quite challenging.

In any case, we should quickly point out that defining man does not involve a stark separation from the rest of things; nor does it determine him as a being that is completely alien or separate from the rest of reality. Certainly, man is different, given that he exhibits characteristics that other beings lack. This does not, however, isolate him, nor does it make him a solitary being, or one so distinct from other beings that nothing similar to him can be found in the environment that

---

[1] Polo dealt with this, in part, in "El sentido cristiano del dolor" (*Obras completas de Leonardo Polo*, v. XIII, Eunsa Pamplona 2015, pp. 139-185). On the same topic, see J. F. Sellés, "Más allá del mal", in *Terrorismo y magnicidio en la historia*, M. Vázquez de Prada (ed.), Eunsa, Pamplona 2008, pp. 17-44.

[2] See J. I. Murillo, "El nacimiento de la antropología griega. Polo y la concepción de Platón sobre el hombre", *Studia Poliana*, 7 (2005) pp. 7-23.

surrounds him; so different that he can find no inspiration or response from the whole of what exists.

The extreme severity of man's distinction with respect to the non-human is more apparent in modern anthropology. But human tragedy is thereby highlighted even more: whoever finds nothing welcoming in the world, nothing like himself, this is the solitary man. The solitude of the human being is not a Greek or classical problem: although man is effectively different from other beings, he maintains at the same time close links with them. This qualification is an important insight and, at the same time, serves as a corrective to the consequences of over emphasizing the difference of man with respect to the rest of reality.

The excessive separation of the determinations of what is human brings negative consequences and carries an unjustified problematic burden. For example: when one interprets the world as completely foreign to the human spirit, as alienation, then human work is understood as a violent attack on nature.

Moreover, this feeling of solitude leads man to subordinate himself to his own works (or to his work) as the only thing in which he can recognize himself. From this comes, for example, the economicism and materialism (of this era)[3].

On the other hand, if one accepts this complete separation, then one must eliminate, along with the accusation of anthropomorphism, any interpretation of things of this world made with categories taken from man (the philosophy of the Greeks contains not a few anthropomorphisms, since it tries to find analogies or similarities with man in these things). For Aristotle, to say, for example, that a dog feels hunger is a valid expression: it correctly reflects what is happening inside the dog. On the other hand, from the point of view of an anthropology that completely isolates man, this expression would be anthropomorphic, and its persistence is rooted in the fact that man is a unique, absolutely solitary, being.

---

[3] See F. Múgica, "El habitar y la técnica: Polo en diálogo con Marx", *Anuario Filosófico*, XXIX/2 (1996), pp. 815-49.

According to this, anthropology nevertheless has a direct value for life, because the attitudes and the development of man's activity depend on how he is understood. Inhabiting a world from which one is distinguished or stands out from, while at the same time maintaining important analogies with it, is not the same as being placed into an absolutely strange world in which there is not even the slightest trace of human qualities.

Greek anthropology makes it clear that man is a being that is distinct from the other beings. However, this difference is not a characteristic that is dialectically opposed to the characteristics of physical reality, nor one that separates man and constitutes him as a solitary being that is foreign to or alienated from the world.

1.2 The Greek definition of man: the animal that has

The Greek definition of man is found (with clarity) in Aristotle, the most completely developed of the Socratic thinkers. It is often said that, for the Stagirite, man is a rational animal; what is common in this definition is the living or animal aspect, and what is peculiar or specific —the difference upon which one should focus on in order to strictly determine what man is— is rationality[4].

Rational animal: this is the usual way of presenting the definition of man in the presentations of this anthropology. However, as I see it, this impoverishes the Aristotelian approach. Man is, indeed, a rational animal, but he is so in a very particular way, which is also reflected in linguistic expression; this needs to be emphasized in order to correctly understand the scope of the Aristotelian definition.

Now, what Aristotle says is that rationality—or any other characteristic—is linked to man, to the human subject, accord-

---

[4] See L. Polo, "La diferencia entre el hombre y el animal" (*Obras completas de Leonardo Polo*, v. XXVI, Eunsa, Pamplona 2018, pp. 29-38).

ing to having[5]. Aristotle does not write that man is a rational animal, but rather that he is an animal that has *logos* or reason. "Having" is the Greek verb *ékhein*. It can be shown, with several of the Stagirite's texts, that what distinguishes man from all other things is having: having reason, having some kind of characteristic, or having things. Man is the being that, unlike others, maintains a relationship of having with his constitutive properties and also with the rest of the world (Aristotle also says that the soul is in a certain way all things: this "in a certain way" is knowledge for whoever possesses it; to be a rational animal is to be capable of possessing everything in the form of an idea or of an object when knowing it). According to this, Greek anthropology directly connects what is constitutional with what is dynamic in man. On the other hand, it is obvious that having does away with ontological solitude and with the subsequent dialectic opposition (between man and what he has).

For the Greeks, what is strictly characteristic of man—and this is worthy today of a lengthy meditation—is having. This is what makes him different from minerals, which, strictly speaking, do not have: they are not possessors of; and it is also what makes him different from plants and animals, which are not possessors either (or are weakly so). God is in no way possessor, but rather Pure Being: He is beyond having. Having is a relation, so to say, and, therefore, is weaker than the being as absolutely perfect, identical with itself in terms of being or that maintains with itself a pure relation of being. Man, on the other hand, is not entirely perfect. Inasmuch as he is a being that has—the phenomenon of having appears in man—, and one that has reason, he is capable of appropriation, which marks out his difference both from what is superior and from what is inferior to him. Having is superior to what is had, although

---

[5] On this topic, see L. Polo, "Tener y dar" (*Obras completas de Leonardo Polo*, v. XIII, Eunsa, Pamplona 2015, pp. 227-253 Also see: J. J. Padial, *La antropología del tener según Leonardo Polo*, Cuadernos de Anuario Filosófico, Serie Universitaria, no. 100, Servicio de Publicaciones de la Universidad de Navarra, Pamplona 2000 and J. Urabayen, "Estudio del tener según Marcel y Polo", *Studia Poliana*, 5 (2003), pp. 199-239.

this superiority is not absolute. But having is, in turn, an indication of a certain indigence, which is manifested in the possibility of losing what is had. One thus sees the appropriateness of approaching anthropology from this classical angle even though the theme of man is not thereby exhausted.

Now, if we characterize man in this way, if we say that what is distinctive in him is not so much that he is rational, but rather something more primary, that is, that he is capable of having, and that he is rational insofar as he has reason (God is not rational, not because he has no reason, but because he is reason, which is not the same), and if this is really the core of classical anthropology just as the Greeks discovered it, then it must be added that they also noted that the relationship of having in man is more or less intense according to the dimensions of his nature. Man is capable of maintaining a relationship of appropriation according to distinct levels (and in the higher levels of this appropriation he comes closer to what in God is strict identity: Being).

The levels of human belonging are threefold[6]. Man is capable of having according to his making and according to his body: this is a first level. Second, man is capable of having according to his spirit, and this is precisely what is rational in man. Finally, man is capable of having in an intrinsic way, or in his very nature, as an acquired perfection. This is what the Greeks call virtue or habit. The capacity to have is precisely what is differential in man, and this human difference is established on three levels. The lowest level is the corporeal-practical level; the intermediate level is what is usually called immanent operation (the notion of immanence points to the greater intensity of cognitive possession with respect to the corporeal-practical possession, which is not immanent); finally, one finds the capacity of human nature for intrinsically having a perfection: virtue. Virtue is what is had by human nature (in itself). Virtues belong to man or he appropriates them in such a way that they come to form part of his very nature. There-

---

[6] On the different levels of possession or having in Greek classical thought see J. F. Sellés, *Antropología para inconformes*, Rialp, Madrid 2007, cap. 2.

fore, virtue is possessed by man in a way that is more radical than that which is ascribed in practice, and it is more perfect because it is not taken away as the corporeal or the rational are; it is a having (virtue) that brings him closer to God and, therefore, to never being alone.

The definition of man in Greek philosophy is developed in a very mature manner by Aristotle. But we can take yet another step more. To the extent that one level is more perfect than another, there is a relationship of subordination such that it is characteristic of the inferior to be a means with respect to the superior, and the superior is thus an end with respect to the inferior. Therefore, it is the same to say: man is a being capable of having (immediately adding that this capacity of having is more or less intense) as it is to draw the following conclusion from the definition: man is a being in which the means-ends relationship is found. Insofar as the capacity of having is exercised on a lower level, it is ordered to an end; this ordering is what is constitutive of what is called means. Man discovers means because he has ends[7].

Thus, as long as there is hierarchy or intensification in the manner of having, the inferior way remains subordinated to the superior one as an instrument. For this reason, man establishes the means-ends relationship, something which also defines him. Bringing the means into relation with the end, understood as the deepest thing that man is capable of, is equivalent to directing life towards ends. It can thus be seen how a definition, which at first sight might seem abstract, presents a great wealth of implications. To more or less appropriate things, to more or less appropriate oneself, implies means-ends relationships. And it is obvious that man is capable of living this relationship. No being inferior to man can do so and, strictly speaking, neither does God, because God does not need means. In God there is no subordination of means to ends; God does so because God does not need means. In God

---

[7] This distinction runs through the whole of medieval philosophy. It involves the distinction between medial goods and the ultimate or final end. Polo refers to this in his book *Ética: hacia una versión moderna de los temas clásicos* (*Obras completas de Leonardo Polo*, v. XI, Eunsa, Pamplona 2018, pp. 141-313).

there is no subordination of means to an end; God is the end of all things, and He is a means for nothing.

On the other hand, this way of understanding man makes it possible to approach his manner of relating himself to his environment through work in a positive manner. It can be said, taking expressions used by His Holiness John Paul II in the Encyclical *Laborem Exercens*, that having formally corresponds to the subjective sense. In contrast, the subordination of man to his works inverts the relative importance of work taken in the subjective sense and taken in the objective sense[8]. The superiority of work in the subjective sense over objective work is of a teleological character, which implies that the act of working is integrated by immanent operations and by virtues, to which its productive efficacy is due. More precisely: the act of working is the channel for the superior forms of possession that are oriented toward the possession and the dominion of the material world. For this reason, work is not a mere mechanical process.

Moreover, the means-ends relation is in a certain way circular. This is because in the order of having, superiority is not absolute (as pointed out earlier). Since the means are impossible without the ends, detaching the latter from the former affects both at the same time. And, since the subjective sense of work is the channel for the relationship, ignorance of it ruins it.

Now, to the extent that man exercises the means-ends relationship, he is master of his practical conduct from his immanent operations, and master of the latter from the virtues. Being master of practical activity and of one's operations—which is possible precisely because man lives according to the means-ends relationship—, this, say the Greeks, is freedom. It is the first sense of freedom. For man, to be free is to be master of his own acts, something which is impossible if the means-ends relationships are not established, if some levels (of having) are not subordinated to others, if some (pos-

---

[8] On this topic, see P. Pintado, "Sobre los sentidos objetivo y subjetivo del trabajo según Polo", *Anuario Filosófico*, XXIX/2 (1996) pp. 949-959.

sessive) acts are not subordinated to others. The capacity of having, synthetically viewed, means, ultimately, freedom. Freedom is the culmination of constitutional anthropology, and in turn is what directs it to dynamic anthropology. Conduct is controllable in accordance with the means-ends relationship that the being capable of having discovers. This is the notion of freedom that Aristotle presents in several places of his work.

1.3 Practical having: means and ends

This being said, we now proceed to the description of each one of the levels of having mentioned above, beginning with the lowest: the corporeal-practical capacity to have. It is precisely here, at this level, that the economy is to be found[9]. For this reason, the economy is merely medial for the Greeks. Economics is practical conduct and corporeal appropriation—properties that refer to the body—. But, as mentioned earlier, if a level of appropriation is less intimate or less intense than another, then it has the character of a means with respect to that other level. Therefore, the level of the economy is the level of means: within it there is nothing but means; the ends are above it. Also, as mentioned above, the connection of the two levels is the act of working. The virtues and the immanent operations are ends of the corporeal-practical actions. The economy, argue the Greeks, is a medial practical activity.

From this follow consequences that are very important for the study of business sciences, which are human sciences. To the extent that this anthropology is correct (as I see it, it is not complete, but it is valid), one must accept that man cannot exercise solely operations of the lower level. The higher levels

---

[9] Polo wrote several unpublished works concerning this science, but references to this topic can be found in the following works: *¿Quién es el hombre?* cap. 5 (*Obras completas de Leonardo Polo*, v. X, Eunsa, Pamplona 2018, pp. 81-89); *Antropología de la acción directiva* (*Obras completas de Leonardo Polo*, v. XVIII, Eunsa, Pamplona 2019, pp. 311-482); and "Ricos y pobres. Igualdad y desigualdad" (*Obras completas de Leonardo Polo*, v. XXV, Eunsa, Pamplona 2015, pp. 303-344; English translation: *Rich and Poor: Equality and Inequality*, Leonardo Polo Institute of Philosophy, South Bend 2017).

are not only ends, but also conditions of possibility for the lower ones. Therefore, the economic activities that belong exclusively to the level of means are capable of being freely exercised. Accordingly, economic laws are neither absolute nor necessary.

It would be dehumanizing to consider the economic mediality as governed by inexorable laws apart from ends, because in that case no freedom would be possible. The economic order is not a necessary order because necessity is in the end. The necessity of the end is compatible with human dignity and with the rising intensity of his possessive capacity. The necessity of the means is conferred. I call the necessity that is commensurate with human need "conferred necessity". Human needs are especially evident in their corporality. Moreover, corporeal-practical possession is inseparable from the problem of man's biological viability. It seems clear that only a body that is not determined as such can open itself to a possessing relationship with things.

Certainly, the means are what they are and, therefore, subject to rules; but they are not autonomous, since they do not constitute a closed realm. Forcing the means' way of being is inseparable from their condition of being means; otherwise they would be means for any end; that is, they could be used regardless of the end. In this sense it is said that the end does not justify the means: the end is not arbitrary. There is nothing in the terminus of pragmatic conduct that is not a means; this being the case, man needs to be capable of directing his conduct toward the higher levels. This thesis is clearly deduced from Greek anthropology, and I believe that it is relevant for the world of business[10].

---

[10] With regard to the topic of business according to L. Polo: "La empresa frente al socialismo y el liberalismo" (*Obras completas de Leonardo Polo*, v. XXV, Eunsa, Pamplona 2015, pp. 279-302); "La interpretación socialista del trabajo y el futuro de la empresa" (*Obras completas de Leonardo Polo*, v. XXV, Eunsa, Pamplona 2015, pp. 345-361); "Las organizaciones primarias y la empresa" (*Obras completas de Leonardo Polo*, v. XXV, Eunsa, Pamplona 2015, pp. 23-191); "Valores dominantes y valores ascendentes en la cultura de la empresa" (*Obras completas de Leonardo Polo*, v. IX, Eunsa, Pamplona 2015, pp. 203-208); "El hombre en la empresa: trabajo y retribu-

Business activity formally consists in the organization of practical activities. Can it be detached from its being a means with respect to higher human levels? Is the teleological neutrality of economic activity acceptable? Greek anthropology says no, because it affects the definition of man. If man is determined to ignore it, he acts like an animal; even more, worse than an animal, because he is forcing his own nature.

The human capacity for having with his body and for actions that configure things, processes, ideas, is what is called technical skill[11]. Man is a technical being because he possesses with his body. Animals never possess with their bodies. Let us look at some examples. Dressing, putting clothing on, is having clothing, say the Greeks. The clothing is had by the body; the body is the measure of the clothing. Thomas Aquinas also points this out. An animal does not have clothing because the skin (with wool, fur, etc.) with which the animal is covered and kept warm is not the ascription of something distinct from its body to its body: it is not a possession, but rather a part of the animal's body itself. For the alpaca this is not clothing, but for me it is. For the alpaca, it does not form part of its body; in contrast, for man it is something ascribed. The human body is defined by establishing relationships of belong with things; for example, Aristotle says, the ring is had; perhaps a ring can be put on an animal, but whatever is placed on the animal is not really had by the animal. On this level many aspects of having appear, which are summarized with the word "inhabit"[12]. Man is the being that inhabits the world. Inhabiting comes from having [*haber*], and having [*haber*] is equivalent to possessing

---

ción" (*Obras completas de Leonardo Polo*, v. XVI, Eunsa, Pamplona 2018, pp. 19-28); "El poder empresarial" (*Obras completas de Leonardo Polo*, v. XVI, Eunsa, Pamplona 2018, pp. 29-35); "La empresa es de todos" in *Capital, negocios y mundo*, Santiago de Chile, 3 (1998); "La ética y las virtudes del empresario", interview with L. Polo by Patricia Pintado (*Obras completas de Leonardo Polo*, v. XXV, Eunsa, Pamplona 2016, pp. 433-445); "Las organizaciones primarias y las empresas" (*Obras completas de Leonardo Polo*, v. XXV, Eunsa, Pamplona 2016, pp. 23-191).

[11] See "Técnica, metafísica y religión" in J.A García and J.J. Padial (eds.) *Autotranscendimiento*, Universidad de Málaga, Málaga 2010.

[12] See F. Múgica, "El habitar y la técnica: Polo en diálogo con Marx", *Anuario Filosófico*, XXIX/2 (1996), pp. 815-849.

[*tener*]. The inhabitant of the world is he who has the world. With such a clear observation regarding the peculiarity of the human body that distinguishes it from other living bodies, Greek anthropology arrives at a conclusion that is very similar to what is revealed in Genesis. Indeed, in the first book of Sacred Scripture, man is the ruler of the world; he is created in order to work and to have dominion over the world[13].

Man is such that he inhabits the world; and inhabiting is having: it is practical having. By being in this house, in this room, I practically ascribe to myself this house or the room. Now (always on the level of the body), there is another way of having, constitutive of inhabiting, which is having productive instruments in the manner of using them. These instruments and their use derive from the constitutive having of inhabiting. This is manual having. Thomas Aquinas comments on this: the only animal with hands is man. It would not be correct to liken a hoof or claw to a hand. A hoof or claw can do anything except have. With a hoof, one can step, strike; with a claw, one can tear. But having (and, by having, fashioning what is had) is possible only with the hand. Having in the hand an instrument called a hammer with which one hammers a nail, or a violin with which one plays a melody, is a corporeal having that becomes possible because man is a being with hands. The hand does not terminate in itself, but rather communicates its dynamism to what it handles. The hand is, as Aristotle said, the instrument of instruments.

Man is also capable of speaking. To speak is to endow with meaning: to deposit a meaning into a sound, and thus to avail-of this meaning in such a way that it can be heard and understood, that is, had: appropriated by another. The being capable of having is the animal with hands; and is, at the same time, and together with this, the speaking animal, the animal of signs. He who has, is, with what he has, capable of referring to another thing. This relationship of reference of one thing to

---

[13] Gn 2:11.

another is a sign. The animal that speaks is, then, the animal that signifies[14].

Here we have a first glimpse of the immense systematic richness of corporeal having: having in the hand, inhabiting, making, using, speaking. Now, another observation can be made. The systematic dimension of practical having consists in the communication of the having to the assortment of what is had. Relationships of co-belonging that are inherent to artifacts thereby arise. He who inhabits has the habitat; the habitat is precisely the correlation between all the things that are in it. Each one of these things refers to others. A set of references exists between these things precisely because they are all had. I have the hammer in the hand; with the hammer I make reference to the nail; the hammer itself is ordered to the nail. The nail is for nailing; nailing is for making the table; the table is also for using. In this way, a plexus of medial references is constituted[15]. And this is the way of being of means.

According to this, the inhabitable world is the plexus of medial references. The Greeks called articulated medial goods *khrémata*, a word from their language that comes from the verb *khrao*, which means "to have in the hand." Heidegger repeats this observation, which is already found in Aristotle, who, in turn, takes it from Protagoras, from whom it originates. We articulate the world because we communicate our having it to it. Things co-belong to each other in our world. There is a relationship between this table and this tray; between this tray and this glass; between the pitcher and the water. All this constitutes a plexus of signifying references that are the inhabitable world. The water is on the tray so that the water does not fall on the table; the table is there to have something to put the tray on, and it was made with nails and a hammer, and of trimmed and cut wood… Now, all this is so, precisely because man has, and by having he communicates, in some

---

[14] See L. Polo, *¿Quién es el hombre?* ch. VIII: El lenguaje y la cultura (*Obras completas de Leonardo Polo*, v. X, Eunsa, Pamplona 2018, pp. 133-155).

[15] Polo deals with the notion of *plexus* in the second lesson of his book *Curso de teoría del conocimiento*, v. II (*Obras completas de Leonardo Polo*, v. V, Eunsa, Pamplona 2016, pp. 45-60).

way, this having to the things that he has, which then come to "have" among each other. A world of medial relationships is thus constituted.

Now, the phenomenon of practical organization makes its appearance here; man is an organizer because he is a possessor[16]. And insofar as he possesses means, he organizes medial plexuses. An animal scurries about, but does not inhabit the world: the world is not his. Now, for the same reason that the world is man's, he communicates his possessing to it, and thus the things that are in the human world refer to each other. Man communicates his character of being possessor in the practical having of instruments to the instruments themselves, and thereby constructs a world of means. The street is for walking or for the car; the stoplight is there for circulation; the house is oriented according to whether or not the Sun rises on this side or that.

What does it mean that man is a technical being? What does it mean that man has hands, or that he is a speaker? All this points to the fact that man always constitutes organizations. Man always orders, because he never does anything in an isolated way: he does something with one thing and for some other thing. The things with which he does things thus come to be connected. Man adds his own organization to the world. For this reason, the theory of society, the theory of technology—which today is called techno-structure—is already based on and is found in the notion of corporeal-practical possession: on the first level of possession[17].

And, according to this, it becomes evident that the world constituted by man—the set of relationships, the referential plexus—is a world in common. It does not exist only for one person, but for a community, given that this plexus is constructed, and is comprehensible, by many. Human society is

---

[16] See L. Polo, "Prologue to J. A. Pérez López, *Teoría de la acción humana en las organizaciones*" (*Obras completas de Leonardo Polo*, v. XVI, Eunsa, Pamplona 2018, pp. 67-69).

[17] Polo refers to these topics in an unpublished work: *Ciencia y sociedad*, Bogotá, 1989.

not a fortuitous event. Man forms societies insofar as he articulates his practical conduct. This articulation is natural, it is inherent to his nature, inasmuch as he is capable of having and of communicating this characteristic to the inhabited world.

Society is based on communication. Human language, says Aristotle, is concerned with what is useful and what is not useful, with what is suitable or not suitable, and also with what is good and evil, what is just and unjust. Here one finds the root of justice, embedded within human relationships precisely because man is a being that possesses, a condition that bestows upon him a title to claim something as his own. The distribution of the plexus does indeed follow certain criteria of function and of use; but it is a priori possible from the perspective of the definition of human nature that we have proposed. The discussion of the criteria for distribution presupposes a title to claim things as his own. Nevertheless, this title is no way exclusive; it cannot be so because the plexus is a whole. A certain number of things are ascribed to each man or to each group; but it must not be forgotten that these things belong to the plexus: they are in it and only within it are they *khrémata*.

Consequently, the idea of absolute private property is a contradiction[18]. Man is an owner precisely because he possesses by nature. But since his form of possessing on the most primary level—the corporeal-constructive-practical level—constitutes a plexus, private property (which is the ascription of a part of the plexus) cannot be carried out by severing the connections of the whole, since it would then loose its meaning. Property is justified by human nature, which is capable of possessing. But this in turn places a limit on the right to property. A person's titles to possess parts of the plexus to the exclusion of others are in principle correct; however, property is not absolute. If the ascription of means implies their complete separation from the order of means as a whole, it would impair and degrade them. And this degradation is reciprocal.

---

[18] Polo takes this up in the unpublished *El derecho de propiedad y la cultura humana*, Urio, 1964.

Thus, the classical approach justifies the structuralist or systematic interpretations of society, which have been in fashion throughout the last few decades. The corresponding sociology is more fundamental than systematic sociology, because the concept of a total system is advantageously replaced by that of the plexus, which turns out to be more flexible. For its part, the concept of subsystem is replaced by preferential criteria of affinity or of intensity; but always without ruining the broader plexus, and without interpreting it according to criteria that are valid only for the subsystems. In the end, the plexus is private and common at the same time.

Correlatively, the community requires comprehension on the part of everyone; people must therefore be given an education. If they are not educated, they become marginalized from the plexus[19]. As Aristotle says, in order to be a citizen, in order to belong to the community, one must know about what is good and what is evil, about what is yours and what is mine, about what is just and what is unjust, about what is useful and what is useless. Consequently, education is not a mere subsystem of social organization[20].

For his part, the citizen is someone who is included and acts in the plexus through or in accordance with his understanding of it. This plexus always exists, even though attention is sometimes not focused on it or it is, but in an inadequate manner due to its being external or partial. The understanding of the practical order is a requirement for the correct exercise of subjective work; its not being understood is a sign of marginalization. From this, various human rights arise; also, in this regard, the distinction between "direct" and "indirect" busi-

---

[19] For more on the Polo's approach to society see F. Múgica, "El pensamiento social de Leonardo Polo", Introduction to *Sobre la existencia cristiana*, Pamplona, Eunsa, 1996, pp. 13-55.

[20] On Polo's theory of education, see L. Polo, *Ayudar a crecer. Cuestiones de filosofía de la Educación* (*Obras completas de Leonardo Polo*, v. XVIII, Eunsa, Pamplona 2019, pp. 141-308.) Also see: F. Altarejos, "Finalidad y libertad en educación", *Anuario Filosófico*, XXIX/2 (1996) pp. 333-345; J. M. Izaguirre and E. R. Moros, *La acción educativa según la antropología trascendental de Leonardo Polo*, Cuadernos de Anuario Filosófico, Serie Universitaria, no. 197, Servicio de Publicaciones de la Universidad de Navarra, Pamplona 2007.

nessmen alluded to by the Pope [ed. note: *John Paul II*] in the aforementioned encyclical is likewise relevant.

According to this, when one so often hears talk of reorganizing or of tearing down structures, one must ask what the plexus is replaced with. This introduces the enormous problem of the modification of the instrumental order; or rather, the question of the history of technology, together with almost all the topics of sociology, both structural as well as dynamic. At least one thing is clear: the pragmatic order cannot arise on a whim. This is not an ideological question, but rather one that is governed by human nature insofar as it is capable of having. For this reason, social reforms, which are oftentimes desirable, give rise to empty social organization and to feeble functionality when they are undertaken carelessly.

Likewise, the connection between the means makes it possible to take notice of the conditional consequences. If one acts, something results from it. This is where the topic of responsibility comes in. A plexus of possible exercisable actions implies freedom of options: I can strike with the hammer, or not; I can drink the water or not drink it; I can use or not use. The plexus offers more possibilities than those that are actualized at any given moment. Medial connections are like threads through which consequences are transmitted. What is done in one area of the plexus is reflected in other areas.

Corporeal-practical possession makes irresponsibility impossible. The irresponsible person stirs up the pot, then goes and hides. He tries to distance himself from the consequences but deceives himself. Someone always suffers the consequences, because everything is intertwined with and related to everything else. Precisely because living together is based on a relational structure, a reciprocal influence among the agents exists. However, actions are frequently undertaken with a view to very specific aims: what is attempted is nothing more than a part of what results. This particular way of acting does not cease being a form of irresponsibility. When one does something, one must consider not only what the agents consider useful for themselves, but also everything that their acts have initiated. For example, if a factory is built next to a river and pollutes the river with waste, then to concern oneself only with the output of the factory is to close off the sphere of the consequences too quickly, since the river forms part of the plexus, and the waste products of the factory that was built affects others—fishermen, for example. This justifies the distinction between "direct" and "indirect" businessmen.

Thus, our world is a world with meaning, imbued with language[21]. Such a world is integrated, moreover, by a process of accumulation that is called tradition. This process is inherent to the objective sense of work and, especially, to productive capital. It is for this reason that these topics are so relevant to business organization. The proposed description makes it clear that the order of means or of practical things is very important, dignified, and peculiar to man; it is not found outside of him. A proof of this is that there is no animal language; animals have nothing but signs of this type. Aristotle says that the animal's voice only expresses its physiological states: shouts of warning, of alarm, of attention, of calling, of anger; it does not refer to what is good and what is unfitting, the just or the unjust, topics which human language deals with.

In any case, the level of means is a human level within which we all find ourselves, including philosophers, even though at times with a certain clumsiness. The first anecdote that the history of philosophy preserves relates that a little Thracian girl laughed at Thales of Miletus, the first philosopher, because he fell into a pit while contemplating the heavens. It is illustrative. But it is also said of him that he bought all the olive oil presses that there were in the market and, when the time came for replacing those that were being

---

[21] The Polian approach to language can be found in these works: *¿Quién es el hombre?* cap. VIII (*Obras completas de Leonardo Polo*, v. X, Eunsa, Pamplona 2016, pp. 133-155); *Nominalismo, idealismo y realismo* (*Obras completas de Leonardo Polo*, v. XIV, Eunsa, Pamplona 2016); *Curso de teoría del conocimiento*, vol. I (*Obras completas de Leonardo Polo*, v. IV, Eunsa, Pamplona 2015, pp. 122-123); *Curso de teoría del conocimiento*, vol. II (*Obras completas de Leonardo Polo*, v. V, Eunsa, Pamplona 2016, pp. 75-83); "Ser y comunicación" (*Obras completas de Leonardo Polo*, v. IX, Eunsa, Pamplona 2015, pp. 181-193; English translation: "Being and Communication", *Journal of Polian Studies* 4 (2017), pp. 7-23).

worn out, he sold them at a very high price. He didn't live in the clouds; and Aristotle adds that Thales did not do anything special, since he simply took advantage of the law of monopoly.

It would be possible to continue the study of having with respect to means; but for the sake of brevity, we should now move on to the explanation of the higher modes of possession.

1.4 Immanent possession: theory and practice

In Plato, as well as in Aristotle, there is the very deep conviction that the level of corporeal-practical having, while very important and peculiar to man, is, nevertheless, not the highest. Above this possession are the so-called immanent operations[22]. These, moreover, are the condition for understanding the practical plexuses and for conducting oneself within them. By immanent operations we mean that human activity according to which man possesses a thing that (upon being possessed) does not remain external, but instead is intrinsic to the possessive operation. In fact, what is thought is possessed in the operation of thinking. I think the concept: what is conceptualized is in my mind, in the very operation of conceptualizing. I do not possess what is thought through my corporality or through my manual skill in the same way that I possess practical things. The immanent operation does not fall

---

[22] Polo studies this type of act extensively and in depth in v. I of his *Curso de teoría del conocimiento, op. cit.* This discovery is distinctly Aristotelian and well developed by his medieval commentators. In this regard, see R. Yepes, *La doctrina del acto en Aristóteles*, Eunsa, Pamplona 1993; D. González Ginocchio, *El acto de conocer. Antecedentes aristotélicos de Leonardo Polo*, Cuadernos de Anuario Filosófico, Serie Universitaria, no. 183, Servicio de Publicaciones de la Universidad de Navarra, Pamplona 2005; J. F. Sellés, *Conocer y amar. Estudio de los objetos y operaciones del entendimiento y de la voluntad según Tomás de Aquino*, 2nd edition, Eunsa, Pamplona 2000; J. I. Murillo, *Operación, hábito y reflexión*, Eunsa, Pamplona 1998. For a study of immanent operations according to Polo, see: H. Esquer, "Actualidad y acto" in *Anuario Filosófico*, XXIX/2 (1996), pp. 145-163; J. M. Posada, "La extratemporalidad del pensar como acto perfecto" in *Studia Poliana*, 1 (1999), pp. 25-58; J. J. Padial, "Las operaciones intelectuales según Polo" in *Studia Poliana*, 2 (2000), pp. 113-144.

back upon what it possesses as something different or external to it, but rather keeps it within itself.

The notion of immanent operation is, undoubtably, a major philosophical discovery. It clearly corresponds to a form of possessing that is more intimate and higher than the previous one. If I see, I have what is seen, says Aristotle. If I think, I have what is thought[23]. But, how do I have what is seen and what is thought? I have what is seen insofar as I see it; I have what is thought insofar as I think it. Man is endowed with a capacity for possessing that gathers from outside and keeps it in front of himself to the same extent that the operation is taking place. Aristotle considers these operations to be more vital than the actions by which technical skill, the dominion of the world, is exercised. The world is possessed more when it is known than when it is acted upon. Theory is superior to practice (understood correctly: as a way of possessing). Without thought, that technical skill would be impossible.

Possession according to thought is more intense than practical possession[24], and for this reason man is defined as a "rational animal". To be rational is to possess intimately. Life always involves an inner realm[25]; but this interiority is not opposed (all the contrary) to the most perfect life opening up to everything in such a way that what it opens up to is had by it. For this reason, the Stagirite writes that the soul is in a certain

---

[23] "When the potencies have as a result some other thing aside from use, its act is in what it is made (for example, building in what is being built…); but, when it has no other work but the act, the act is in the agent itself (for example, vision in he who sees)." Aristotle, *Metaphysics* Bk. IX, ch. 8 (BK 1050 a 30-246). In addition to this text, see: *On the Soul*, Bk. III, ch. 4 (BK 929 b 25-26); ch. 7 (BK 431 a 4-7); ch. 8 (BK 431 b 20-28); ch. 10 (BK 433 b 22-27); *Physics*, Bk. III, ch. 3 (BK 202 a 13-14), etc.

[24] A Thomistic commentary states: "so, the practical arts are ordered to the speculative ones, and likewise every human operation is ordered to intellectual speculation, as an end." Thomas Aquinas, *Summa Contra Gentiles*, Bk. III, ch. 25, n. 9.

[25] In this regard, see Polo's *Lecciones de psicología clásica* (*Obras completas de Leonardo Polo*, v. XXII, Eunsa, Pamplona 2015).

way all things: *psykhé pôs pánta*²⁶. This *pôs*, "in a certain way", refers to the immanent operation.

Now, if man produces in order to satisfy bodily needs, and if production presupposes theory as a condition of possibility, then it will have to be concluded that man is not viable without intelligence²⁷. Seen from this perspective, the importance of work lies in its already mentioned value as a channel for theoretical reason towards its practical use²⁸. A stamp of unity between spirit and nature in man. Corporeal-practical possession certainly presupposes man's biological indigence and comes to be its remedy. But formulating it apart from knowledge is a circular argument. Moreover, man's end is not mere survival.

In the final analysis, a practical world is organized because it is first known. Men, in turn, gather together in society because they know how to speak²⁹. And because they know how to speak, they know how to make. Speech is an outwardly direct communication that presupposes knowing. From this one can conclude that the end of all practical activities is the better exercise of immanent operations. A surprising conclusion at first glance; but inevitable. Man constructs a world so as to better carry out cognitive operations (and the other way around: greater knowledge increases constructive capacity). Man's end is not production, but rather contemplation³⁰; and

---

²⁶ Aristotle, *On the Soul*, Bk. III, ch. 8 (BK 431 b 21); *ibid*, Bk. III, ch. 5 (BK 430 a 14 ff.).

²⁷ This topic is further developed in chapter II of Polo's *Etica: hacia una versión moderna de los temas clásicos*, Madrid (*Obras completas de Leonardo Polo*, v. XI, Eunsa, Pamplona 2018, pp. 169-189).

²⁸ See L. Polo, *Ricos y pobres*, ch. 6: "Conocimiento y trabajo" (*Obras completas de Leonardo Polo*, v. XXV, Eunsa, Pamplona 2015, pp. 337-338); I. J. Engonga Ona, *El trabajo según Leonardo Polo*, Licentiate thesis, Ecclesiastical School of Philosophy, Universidad of Navarra, Pamplona 2003.

²⁹ On the topic of society, see L. Polo, "La 'sollicitudo rei socialis': una encíclica sobre la situación actual de la humanidad" (*Obras completas de Leonardo Polo*, v. XIII, Eunsa, Pamplona 2015, pp. 255-315). Also see C. Naval, "En torno a la sociabilidad humana en el pensamiento de Polo", *Anuario Filosófico*, XXIX/2 (1996) pp. 869-883.

³⁰ This thesis is classical. See, for example: J. F. Sellés, *Razón teórica y razón práctica según Tomás de Aquino*, Cuadernos de Anuario Filosófico, Serie Universitaria,

production is worthwhile to the extent that it is a means for something higher. Man is *Homo faber* because he his *Homo sapiens*; he is *Homo sapiens* more than he his *Homo faber*, and he is *Homo faber* so as to be *Homo sapiens*[31]. Contemplation is more important than production.

Can all this be said to persons involved in business, to people dedicated precisely to production? Yes. It's more: it should be said. Everything that we do in this world has understanding as its end (understanding and loving, because loving too is a perfect operation. Although the Greeks were not able to completely see the latter; it is a discovery of Christian anthropology[32]. Christianity considers loving to be a strictly vital activity; the Greek formula is thus completed: having and giving)[33]. Everything we do, if it is not useful for knowing and for loving, lacks meaning. Man is free only when he establishes this relationship of means to ends. Obviously, knowledge can be applied: science has a technical use. But this use, in turn, demands in return a new intellectual aptitude and a better love. Without this, the technical world—which is already human because it is made by man—becomes inhuman.

As mentioned, man humanizes the world through his inhabiting. But he can also destroy it. That is where we find, for example, neutron bombs that leave human works intact, but which annihilate life. If humanity were swept away by these bombs, the plexus of civilization would be left in a state of paralysis. It would be a plexus without subjects: anonymous, indifferent; a world that has lost its human dimension precisely because of the absence of men who live in it and who carry it forward.

---

no. 101, Pamplona Servicio de Publicaciones de la Universidad de Navarra, Pamplona 1999.

[31] In this regard, see: L. Polo, *Ética, op. cit.*, cap. 1 (*Obras completas de Leonardo Polo*, v. XI, Eunsa, Pamplona 2018, pp. 141-167).

[32] See Sellés's book mentioned earlier: *Conocer y amar, op. cit.*, cap. II.

[33] Polo discusses this this in "Tener y dar" (*Obras completas de Leonardo Polo*, v. XIII, Eunsa, Pamplona 2015, pp. 227-253).

It is of great importance to realize that the economy is an activity proper to man. But it is also important to be aware that it is a means, and that its human value is obtained only by virtue of immanent operations. Today we have what is often called "free time" and, as technology advances, we have increasingly more of it. Free time highlights the problem of the finality of practical activity. If this problem is not solved, then instead of free time we will have to speak of empty time. A civilization that is not aware of this problem builds a technological world that slips through man's grasp and thus becomes inhuman.

Strictly speaking, the truth has no useful substitute[34]. Practical life is based on truth, and has as its end progress in the acquisition of the truth. If our works are not controlled from the truth, they then, precisely because of this, slip out of our control. This is the situation in which we find ourselves. Forces that have a frightful appearance are emerging from the world that we have created. If there is no wisdom in world leaders, how is the risk of self-destructive wars to be managed? How is the so-called North-South dialogue to be carried forward? If the means-ends relationship is inverted, then *homo faber* is transformed into the "sorcerer's apprentice", and then there appears the tragic character of technology, which upon being emptied of human meaning, is transformed into our enemy.

Do we control technology today? No. Why not? Because we have paid attention exclusively to the results of manufacturing. This is neither a cliché nor a loss, but rather the simple truth. The signs that I describe of our works slipping from our grasp, of the world that we have constructed becoming uninhabitable, is obviously related to problems of justice, which need to be carefully analyzed. From this point of view, it is enough, for example, to consider the question of Latin Ameri-

---

[34] "Strictly speaking, the truth has no useful substitution. Practical life rests on the truth, and has as its end progress in the acquisition of the truth. If they are not controlled from the truth, our works will, precisely because of this, slip away from our grasp." (L. Polo, *Obras completas de Leonardo Polo*, v. XIII, Eunsa, Pamplona 2015, p. 238).

ca's foreign debt with North American banks. The debtor-creditor relationship is a very important plexus. The following questions must then be asked: What type of activity does a banker carry out? For what type of activity was the credit requested? Was it carried out, or not? What is, in general, the relationship between financial capitalism and industry? The analytical elements needed to address this problem are contained within our approach.

Another aspect of this dissociation—works are escaping our control—is the discordance between work and capital[35]. But these are not the only risks of dehumanization that are inherent to our technological situation; those risks are quite extensive. Within a growing number of sectors of technology, the situation is such that, instead of us being the ones who mark out the path for the instrument, it is the product that demands our dedication, that co-opts our activity in accordance with a configuring structure of action that is imposed by the instrument itself. Our behavior, under these conditions, follows the product's dynamic.

An instrument—like a hammer, for example—is a prolongation of human corporality that can be activated. McLuhan insists on this idea: in accordance with his possibilities of configuration, man produces instruments that are like prolongations that were already prefigured in him (a hammer is the external replica of the fist). As long as these prolongations are within our action, as long as they are possessed by them, we possess and have dominion over the instrumental plexuses. Now, if the instrument becomes defiant, if it imposes its own dynamic, and if it obliges us to follow it, then it is unlikely that a result useful to man will be obtained from using it. For this reason, we cannot allow technology to get out of hand. However, this can happen in the situation in which we find ourselves. Man can be superseded by the technological exo-organism inasmuch as it can become impossible to adapt his own corporeal being to it: here the technological exo-

---

[35] In this regard, see L. Polo, *La empresa es de todos* (*Obras completas de Leonardo Polo*, v. XVI, Eunsa, Pamplona 2018, pp. 227-229).

organism functions as it drags man's corporeal being along and overruns it. If we do not direct the machines, we become their slaves; this is neither an accident, nor a science fiction story; rather it is starting to happen. And it is one of the more common risks of the present technological situation.

If technology functions on its own or automatically, then we are incorporated into it as its products, and no longer as agents. This alternative is a moral problem. It seems clear that in order to face this problem, considering the organization of work is not enough; nor is the "reproduction" of the structure of this organization or its changes enough. It is necessary to address the question of technology's historical changes as a function of the quantity of scientific knowledge that is incorporated into it. Thus, for example, a hierarchy of technologies is established in accordance with the incorporated knowledge. Furthermore, the question of adapting different types of technologies to different human capabilities is of the highest importance. This is the task of the so-called "appropriate" technology; that is, one that is suitable to the situation of the men who use it.

Marx said that man creates the conditions of his physical existence through his work. Marx's anthropology moves exclusively on the level of means, which he confuses with ends (for Marx, theory is praxis). Marxism is anachronistic on its own level of conditions, because its function between the means and the ends makes it incapable of facing the threat contained in today's technology. For this reason, the Marxism of the last few decades of the twentieth century followed a strictly tragic line, as can be seen in Adorno and Bloch. The Marxist idea that man, by producing, constructs his own physical existence in this world is rather simple. But if this is taken as the key to history and as the goal of man, then how are we to face the rebellion of technology? I understand that there are still Marxists in Latin America[36]. Wouldn't they be neo-

---

[36] Polo's (still unpublished) licentiate thesis, directed by Prof. Pérez Ballester, professor of logic at the University of Barcelona, is titled *La antropología de Marx*. Also see "Marxismo y Sociedad" (*Obras completas de Leonardo Polo*, v. XXX Eunsa,

indigenist enemies of technology instead? In any case, this would be an incoherent adoption of basic Marxist ideology.

We are producing our physical existence in the world; yes, but, are we building a human world[37]? Are we maintaining our power over technology as means? In this regard, I usually propose what I have said: that the way to prevail over the risk of autonomous technology's dehumanization is to admit that contemplation is superior to action[38], and to procure control of technology. But also, that the subject of this control cannot be any other but business[39]. Among the responsibilities that belong to business at this historical moment, the first, as I see it, is the control of technology. A business system that is pulled along behind technology leads to the destruction of the medial practical plexus. Controlling technology does not mean, of course, putting a stop to it, but rather applying it in accordance with the possibilities of human use. There is no danger of stopping because, ultimately, man is the author of technology. But its use must be correctly determined, taking into account the circumstances of the situation and, as I say, also human capacity's effective degree of development in each case.

Technology should be esteemed because technology is human. But it can sometimes happen that it escapes from our grasp. This might be why many present-day views concerning technology's leading role are expressed in exaggerated or excessively rigid theses. I believe that the only social agent capable of refuting this anti-humanist thesis is business. Philosophers are insistent. We want to express ideas that are difficult to spread. But it seems to me that it is important to speak of this to those who have dedicated themselves to the

---

Pamplona 2012, pp. 185-196) and the still unpublished *Aspectos fundamentales del pensamiento de Marx*.

[37] In this regard, see Polo's "Modalidades del tiempo humano" (*Obras completas de Leonardo Polo*, v. XIII, Eunsa, Pamplona 2015, pp. 49-62).

[38] Polo that refers to this in "Acción y contemplación" (*Obras completas de Leonardo Polo*, v. XXX, Eunsa, Pamplona 2012, pp. 361-366).

[39] Because business is a human institution, not a technological means. See L. Polo, *La empresa frente al socialismo y el liberalismo* (*Obras completas de Leonardo Polo*, v. XXV, Eunsa, Pamplona 2015, pp. 279-302).

important task of directing businesses. They are ideas that directly touch upon the clarification of the businessman's function. Anthropology is not a science for show or ornamentation, because it deals with the truth concerning man, which is sometimes of a tragic nature. The technological world can be tragic. But before that, it is strictly human, because it is the development of one of man's defining characteristics.

1.5 Habits: growth and cybernetics

Let us now move on to the presentation of man's third possessive level, which is habit, virtue. The concept of virtue can be understood from the perspective of the cybernetic interpretation of the immanent operation[40]. The exercise of spiritual immanent operations results in feedback in its principle, that is, in the principle of these acts: it modifies the structure of the faculty, either perfecting it or making it worse. The perfecting of the faculty as a consequence of the exercise of its acts is virtue[41]; the imperfection that comes about as a consequence of a defective exercise is vice. The virtues are called intellectual if they perfect the intelligence and moral if they perfect the tendencies. The moral virtues, as the perfecting of human tendential qualities, reinforces them in such a way that they, in turn, allow the entry of freedom or its intensification in the use of these tendencies.

The cybernetic approach helps in the understanding of the Aristotelian concept of habit, of virtue (or of vice). From this point of view, we pass from the level of immanent opera-

---

[40] This theme is presented by Polo in "La cibernética como lógica de la vida" (*Obras completas de Leonardo Polo*, v. XXVI, Eunsa, Pamplona 2017, pp. 19-28).

[41] Polo deals with the theme of virtue in his *Ética*, cap. IV. (*Obras completas de Leonardo Polo*, v. XI, Eunsa, Pamplona 2018, pp. 211-247). For people in business some references to virtues are offered in "La ética y las virtudes del empresario", an interview by Patricia Pintado Mascareño with L. Polo, *Atlántida*, 14 (1993) pp. 80-92. Polo also deals with this topic in "Las virtudes del empresario (fortaleza y templanza)" (*Obras completas de Leonardo Polo*, v. XXX, Eunsa, Pamplona 2022, pp. 465-486); "La conexión sistémica de las virtudes" (*Obras completas de Leonardo Polo*, v. XXX, Eunsa, Pamplona 2022, pp. 487-525); and "Las virtudes morales" (*Obras completas de Leonardo Polo*, v. XXX, Eunsa, Pamplona 2022, pp. 553-557).

tion to that of habits, since an operation is a means to virtue. If an operation is exercised, feedback is produced: the structure of the faculty is modified, and the next act is better or worse. By working, man is either ennobled or debased. From this, the primacy of the subjective sense of work over its objective sense also follows. Virtue is a value that is superior to utility.

I proposed this way of understanding virtue following professor Pérez López, who made brilliant use of it. From the functional point of view (and in formal terms), man is considered as a set of operational variables. Any human activity is explained in this way. The pragmatic level is the result of the functioning of the set of the variables. I will call it R. Now, we must keep in mind that the set of variables has functioned: the system formed by this set has been modified; if we call this C, then in strict complication with R the system passes from C to C'.

In a valuation of objectives, one must attend to R and to C'. A factory is a set of variables that functions. In a shoe factory, R are the shoes and C' is what has happened to those who make the shoes precisely insofar as they make them. If the set of variables has deteriorated, then C' is negative; if it has gotten better, then C' is positive. It is very important to decide if the modification of C is subordinated to R, or the other way around. If the latter, then C' is the end. It is a form of very grave irresponsibility to reduce the valuation of objectives to R (Pérez López calls the measure of R efficacy and C' efficiency. The correlation of both is the consistency of the system).

This cybernetic interpretation is valid with respect to each individual, and also for the functioning of a business and of any human institution. R must be at the service of the optimal deployment of C. The positive or negative modification of C inevitably derives both from conduct and immanent operations. And from this modification a new form of activity follows. There is an operative gain of virtue: acts engender virtues and virtues make new acts possible.

In order to improve practical activity, it is usual to consider only what is called learning, which is often times interpreted in a behaviorist sense or in terms of conditioned reflexes. Learning is similar to virtuous habits but strictly speaking it is not a virtue, nor does it go beyond the level of means. For this reason, it is related with the concept of "manpower", with the formation of specialists or of experts in engineering skills. More than being an objective of the organization, it is one of its requirements, since it marks out the aptitude for certain tasks. The consistency of R and C through mutual reinforcement is weak in learning and clear in virtue. On the other hand, the functional appearance of virtues in the plexus points to its human value. For example: work relationships based on friendship are completely different from work relationships based on enmity (friendship is a virtue; enmity a vice). The structure of Japanese industry is based on a series of traditional virtues that reinforce R in a surprising way. What kind of virtues are active in a Japanese business? Perhaps they are feudal virtues that guarantee a quasi-political allegiance: faithfulness and fulfillment of one's work as a duty, because this work is integrated into a management style that is not interested solely in work, but also in other dimensions of the subject. They are not the only virtues possible. Freedom, as a Westerner understands it, yields more directly creative virtues (with the alternative being vices ranging from vital discontinuity to the interpretation of human existence as a series of disconnected endeavors). In any case, the acceptance of effort as one's own, without discharging it upon another (seeking, in turn, equal share) is a virtue. An industry works much better this way than when its components "pass the buck".

1.6 Knowledge and virtue as the culmination of life

Let us summarize. Greek anthropology, in its most mature form, defines man by establishing his differential character: man is the being that can have. The being capable of having is not just a thing. Neither is it God who, as strict identity with himself, is beyond having. Man is therefore an intermediate being, above mere physical beings and below the divinity.

Now, the capacity to have is open to analysis, because man does not always possess in the same way. Since it involves having ontologically considered, this distinct manner is hierarchical: one has in one way or another according to the intensity by which one has. It is neither a quantitative difference, nor only relative to that which is had, but rather it is due to the way of having.

On the other hand, whenever a difference is hierarchical—especially, if it is found in the same being—, a dependency exists: the inferior depends on the superior. And, with regard to activities, this dependency is expressed according to the "means-ends" formula: inferior having has the characteristic of being means with respect to the superior way of having. Aristotle distinguishes three levels of having as activity that defines man. The first level is making, corporeal-practical having. Man is an inhabitant because he constructs the world. Making is constructive: it gives rise to configurations, to artifacts. But that is not all. Because it is a having, making communicates its own capacity for having to the artifacts and, therefore, the artifacts "have" each other, they refer to each other according to a reference that, making use of a word employed by the translators of Heidegger, I call "plexus". In *Being and Time*, this ancient idea of having is repeated: the interpretation of man begins there, looking to pragmatic activity.

The second level is immanent possession, which is characteristic of cognitive operations. Unlike making, cognitive operations are not activities that come to an end outside, nor are they exercised with respect to a pre-existing substrate that it shapes or reshapes. Immanent operations do not go outside of themselves, but rather, in contrast, present or lay out that which is possessed upon possessing it (for this reason they are of knowledge). Understanding has that which is understood. Color, insofar as it is being seen, is had by the act of seeing it. This is knowledge's way of having objects. The word "object" is sometimes interchanged with the word "thing". Here, it is used as contra-distinct from thing: object is precisely what is possessed by the cognitive immanent operation.

Now, immanent operations are superior to practical activity. From the point of view of having, having objects is more than having things. This does not mean that the known object is more important than the thing. However, the immanent possession of things is impossible. The immanent operation corresponds with known objects. In contrast, the possession that the human body is capable of in its "poietic" or pragmatic deployment is weaker, and corresponds with the "things of life", which the Greeks called *khrémata* or *pragmata*: tools and tasks in general. This type of things, defined by their non-immanent human possession, are indispensable for life: they are not, strictly speaking, physical entities. On the other hand, the indispensable should not be confused with what is most noble. The indispensable is that without which man could not survive or would be left in a situation of being left adrift in the universe.

Man dwells in his own world to the same extent that he builds this set of ordered things through relationships of a medial nature, each with respect to each other. Precisely because the means are interrelated—this is the order of the means—, they are not things in the absolute sense, that is, mere physical entities. Reality insofar as absolute cannot be had in a practical way. On the other hand, the immanent operation is only possible with regard to the absolute of the real. For this reason, although human knowledge does not possess the real absolutely, it possesses an absolute dimension of it which is called truth[42]. This explains why the plexus ordered by medial relationships is subordinated to knowledge that, in its highest form, is usually called contemplation (with a not completely accurate translation of the Greek word theory).

---

[42] Polo presents the absolute dimension of human *truth*, as well as the *axiomatic* character of human knowledge in his *Curso de teoría del conocimiento*, I-IV *Obras completas de Leonardo Polo*, vv. IV-VII, Eunsa, Pamplona 2015-2019), especially in volume I.

Theory, says Aristotle, is the highest form of life[43]. Even then, we human beings exercise it in an intermittent manner. God always exercises it, and He thus exists as pure intelligence. This is the notion proposed by Aristotle in Book XII of the *Metaphysics*: an intellectual living being: pure theory. Man is not pure theory: but insofar as he exercises it, there is something divine within him. It is therefore clear that theory is above practice. The Stagirite is right. Nevertheless, something that he did not consider needs to be added, namely, that—as mentioned—the will is also capable of perfect or teleological operations. And this is a Christian discovery.

As long as practical activity is a means, it is inferior to theory[44]. Man makes, ultimately, so as to be in the conditions—so to say—to do nothing from the point of view of configuration. This is the relationship between business (*necotium*) and leisure (*otium*): business is the negation of leisure. Leisure in no way means laziness, but rather being free: free from the urgencies of life in order to dedicate oneself to the most noble activity, which is theory. Galileo said that theory is the captain, and practical activity the soldier. To what is superior there corresponds a hegemonic value, a directive function well expressed in Galileo's comparison.

This conviction—that to a large extent we owe to the Greeks—has been taken up in its entirety by Christian civilization, even to the point of having institutionalized it. Strictly speaking, the only civilization that cultivates knowledge institutionally, the only one for which knowledge is, therefore, one of the factors of its own historical trajectory, is precisely Western civilization. Universities are the institutionalization of this classical idea, the leaven for the only culture that is ruled by the motto: we must increase the flow of our knowledge, in the form of a collective task, as one of the most important factors of social dynamics. The high regard for ideas led to science. This gave rise to and nourished the great task of research without which the West is incomprehensible. And since theory

---

[43] See Aristotle, *Nicomachean Ethics*, Bk. X, ch. 7 (BK 1178 a 6-7).
[44] See J. F. Sellés, *Razón teórica y razón práctica, op. cit.*

enriches practice, the West is also a great pragmatic civilization.

However, the two lines of progress are frequently disassociated from each other in the perceptions of individuals and of social groups. For this reason, men who focus on the practical are surprised to see that people are moved by ideas, and that these ideas influence their affairs. What is happening here? Which of the discordant elements has disappeared? What do ideas have to do with the corporate world, with businesses? It is clear that they have something to do with them, and that they favor or disturb them. This is another characteristic of Western society.

For their part, it has already been pointed out that the Greeks were perceptive enough to notice that there is yet another form of possession that follows immanent operations, the principle of which is immaterial. This derivation indicates that the immanent operation is, in its own way, a means to the habits[45]: it is not at all what is highest in man. Immanence is neither what is most intimate, nor what is most radical in him. An improvement or worsening of its principle always follows from it. And this connection to a consequence that goes beyond it also points to its dignity. The immanent operation is open upward and downward: it is sufficiently rooted to direct practical activity, but, at the same time, it leads to interior enrichment.

Practical possession is finite and, because of its weakness, is subject to loss and to change: we put on or take off a piece of clothing; we enter and exit a store. This connects with fashions and styles, temporal or particular forms that give nuance to practical configurations and their historicity. Immanent possession, because it is more intense, is not a question of taking off and putting on, because although it is not always exercised, it leaves a mark in the subjectivity: something more

---

[45] See S. Collado, *Noción de hábito en la teoría del conocimiento de Polo*, Eunsa, Pamplona 2000; J. F. Sellés, "Los hábitos intelectuales según Polo", *Anuario Filosófico*, XXIX/2 (1996) pp. 1017-1036; J. F. Sellés, *Los hábitos intelectuales según Tomás de Aquino*, Eunsa, Pamplona 2008.

than a fashion or a style. This mark, which always follows from the operation, is, for its executing principle, virtue[46] or, if it is negative, vice.

The operations are therefore ordered to the virtues, which in this sense are what really perfect man. For this reason, virtue is the point where having makes contact with the being of man, the conjunction of the dynamic and the constitutional. Man is not always theorizing; on the other hand, virtue is permanent: it remains incorporated in a stable manner; it goes beyond the condition of exercise or non-exercise in which the immanent operations remain. Divine intellection is eternal; human intellection is not eternal, but rather sporadic. Anthropology errs if it takes the rational in man to be absolute. This interpretation obscures the consideration of virtue and, for the same reason, neither does it correctly frame the articulation of what is constitutional and what is dynamic in man. Virtue is a stable disposition: it becomes incorporated into the being of the one who has it. For this reason, it is said that it is a "second nature". From the perspective of virtue, man is the beneficiary of his own activity, or also the victim, if his activity is wrong.

Moreover, that is where one finds the key to tragic anthropology, which is, in turn, obscured if reason is made absolute. The tragic in man consists in wanting to limit himself with impunity to harming others or to failing with regard to the truth, which is impossible, because it is prevented by that peculiar feedback by which our acts determine us. Socrates said that it is worse to commit injustice than to suffer it[47], because in the first case we make ourselves unjust and not in the second: whoever suffers injustice "has a rough time"; but

---

[46] See J. F. Sellés, *Hábitos y virtud*, I-III, Cuadernos de Anuario Filosófico, Serie Universitaria, numbers 65 to 67, Servicio de Publicaciones de la Universidad de Navarra, Pamplona 1999; *Los hábitos adquiridos. Las virtudes de la inteligencia y de la voluntad según Tomás de Aquino*, Cuadernos de Anuario Filosófico, Serie Universitaria, number 118, Servicio de Publicaciones de la Universidad de Navarra, Pamplona 2001.

[47] "The greater evil is not suffering injustice, but committing it." (Plato, *Gorgias*, 474 c ff.).

whoever commits it "becomes evil". To disregard C' and to worry about R, about the external result, is pure superficiality.

The human subject benefits from that type of rebound by which its operating is incorporated into itself in the form of virtue. Therefore, selfish objectives are, in the end, contradictory. Man attains his own benefit, the truly intrinsic one, not by proposing it as a faraway and different or external goal—because it is not—, but rather as something added that is due to the very way of being of his possessive nature. The end in man's essence is virtue. But it cannot be directly achieved, because it is not an object or a thing, but rather is in the intimacy of man: this is where it is acquired as a benefit added to the proper exercise of one's active endowment.

Accordingly, selfishness is a superfluous and misguided aspiration. Without ignoring what is tragic in the human condition, it must be admitted that man is capable of correct action, which is measured in terms of truth and of beneficial contribution towards one's neighbor. But to this same extent, man is also capable of improving. Both results are inseparable. Therefore, neither "egoism" nor "philanthropism" nor "virtuoism" are correct, because they are one-sided. The social and virtue are inseparable[48], because the end of living together is the goodness of living. The active exercise of our nature does not aim at isolated linear objectives, but rather to a joint and complex objective.

On the other hand, man is also distinguished from animals in this respect. An animal cannot receive from its own nature that prize which is called virtue. In terms of perfection, human nature is also an end in itself. For this reason, man cannot be understood as a stage in the evolutionary series of life forms. And for this reason too, the proposal of "self-realization", as if man were an artifact, does not make much sense. The good must be done; but it is shortsighted to consider oneself as an objective without taking into account that it is one's own nature that is in charge of self-finalizing itself,

---

[48] Polo deals with the so-called "social virtues" in *¿Quién es el hombre?*, cap. VII (*Obras completas de Leonardo Polo*, v. X, Eunsa, Pamplona 2016, pp. 111-131).

something which completely excludes the end of human nature from being a technical matter.

Thus, an anthropology that does away with the notion of virtue is deficient and pessimistic. The study of the human capacity of possessing is cut short if it is reduced to a single level. Nor is virtue the last word[49]; but anthropology is to a large extent decided here. Do we accept the thesis that as a consequence of its acts, human nature is capable of a perfecting along the same line, or do we pay attention exclusively to verifiable experimental results ("tangible results", as they say)? We can possess the "tangible result", but only with the hand. Are we content with having the good—no matter how great—only in the hand?

Moreover, the reference to the practical plexus is found to be subject to all types of contingencies. From this point of view, human life is very precarious: success is possible, but so is failure. And, on the other hand, who can take virtue away? Virtue is a possession that is so stable that, I insist, human nature and its actuation coincide in it. Clarity on this point is of great importance when it comes to orientations or attitudes towards life. Much is put on the line here. If the range of possessions is reduced to manual possessions, then human impoverishment is very grave. Happiness has been given up for good.

The goal of life, says Aristotle, is happiness. And this consists in the possession of what is most adequately fitting without fear of losing it. Possessing and losing: why can something be lost? For two reasons: either because what is possessed is corruptible, or because one lacks sufficient strength of adherence. Now, even the capacity to adhere completely is characteristic of virtue. Therefore, whoever does not have virtues cannot be happy. He will not, perhaps, lack what

---

[49] Virtue perfects human *essence*. But the human *act of being* is superior to the essence. In this regard, recall the Thomistic real distinction between *actus essendi* and *essentia*. According to Polo, the innate habits (synderesis, first principles and wisdom) mediate between the act of being and the essence. The human act of being is elevated by other "habits" that are neither innate, nor acquired, but rather infused. These are the *supernatural virtues* (faith, hope, and charity).

makes him happy; but it will be him who fails the felicitous good: it is he himself who will not be faithful to it. The perfect possession of what makes one happy requires the strength of human adherence, solidity, the constancy of our nature. And without virtue we are inconsistent and inconstant.

Moreover, virtue prepares a new actuation. It can be said that virtue is the human factor of hyperformalization. The perfecting of the faculty is, furthermore, its strengthening. Consequently, hyperformalization broadens the scope of what is possible: it makes possible that which in a previous state was not possible. For this reason, human life is not a serial process, as, for example, positivists understand it: if A, then B; if B, then C. That is, from A, B and C follow successively. In man's case, insofar as he is a hyperformal functional system, this is not the case; rather, A makes B possible, and B makes C possible; but it cannot be said that A makes C possible, because only the formal increase achieved from B opens up the possibility of C. There is a situation C that is impossible from situation A and, yet, not completely impossible.

This observation is important when it comes to the calculation or forecasting of objectives starting from any given situation. What is foreseen as feasible from some starting point is ordinarily not much, because as long as a new point of departure has not been attained, the horizon of possibilities is narrow. This renewal of initiative—from what is initial—is what is characteristic of hyperformalization. While taking into account the available resources, calculation presents certain projects as possible; and it also states that the increase of resources would allow other more ambitious projects to be undertaken. Calculation, however, counts on what is given; hyperformalization is something else: it is not an increase of resources, but innovation in the principle of the acts. Thus, if theory is the captain and practical activity is the soldier, then virtue would fittingly be called the general. The general is the hyperformalization of man's spiritual faculties: intelligence and will. Hyperformalization is what is anti-mechanical in man; the overcoming of initial conditions.

Is it possible for man to attain the goals that he sets for himself? The negative response must not be the last word: true, today I am unsuccessful; but it is not right to disregard one's hyperformalization (and that of one's collaborators) by which a path that is at present unsuspected is opened up, because it entails a novelty in my way of being: a perfecting of one's own nature. This is important for any assessment of objectives. Virtue also has a perfective character from the point of view of practicable objective goals—or rather, on the practical level—: for example, those of a businessman. These objectives are never completely predictable, but neither must they be taken as closed: they are not fixed.

2. Giving: Notes on Christian Anthropology

2.1 Desiring and loving: "operosity" of love and hyperteleology

The concept of virtue marks the point of contact between Greek and Christian anthropology[50]. It is the summit of the former and, so to speak, the channel of the second. For its part, the virtue in which the course of the Christian life is best shown is hope[51]. Hope is linked to love: it arises from it and is directed to it. These considerations frame the central themes of existence and of the human person.

Greek anthropology is correct in its basic outline, but it is not complete: it does not inquire into some important human themes. If from Greek philosophy a high ideal of human nature is obtained, the discovery of the dignity of man is, strictly speaking, Christian, not pagan. The great Socratic philosophers are, among the pagan philosophers, the most humanistic; but, next to what can be called Christian "theandrism" this philosophy falls behind. Strictly speaking,

---

[50] In this regard, see L. Polo "Ética socrática y moral cristiana" (*Obras completas de Leonardo Polo*, v. XVI, Eunsa, Pamplona 2018, pp. 127-145).

[51] Leonardo Polo studied this virtue in "Coexistencia, libertad y esperanza" (*Obras completas de Leonardo Polo*, v. XVIII, Eunsa, Pamplona 2019, pp. 112-119).

Christianity is not only humanistic, it is theandric: divine-human.

Even without a deep exposition of this concept, it should be made clear that the meaning of Christianity is completely distorted when the man-God relationship is established as its fundamental truth. Christianity is not primarily an androtheism, but rather the opposite: what is primary is the God-Man relation, the Incarnation[52]. The idea of the divinization of man, of the entrance of the human into the divine sphere appears in myths or, at least, in a phase of the development of the mythic mode of knowledge. But on this point, Christianity is strictly anti-mythical (the relationship of Biblical Revelation to myth is an interesting topic, but this is not the place to explain this). Christianity is not mere humanism, nor primarily the deification of man (which follows as a consequence); what is primary, what is revealed news, is the Incarnation of God.

Now, what is the rationale for theandricism, for the existence of God made man? It cannot be anything but love. Because of that, Christianity comes into play in a completely novel way—I will not say revolutionary, because the notion of revolutionary Christianity has become rather tarnished by liberation theology—: it comes into play as something absolutely unsuspected and unexpected. This what St. John literally expresses: God is Love[53].

Christianity knows that God is Love. And theandricism, which is the radical proposal concerning the theme of man in Christianity, is only possible if God is Love. God does not become man out of any necessity, nor out of any desire; in no way whatsoever does He need to become incarnate. It entails a pure bestowal; perfect ontological generosity[54]. Certainly, "inwardly" God is Love: Love of Himself. But God also loves outwardly; and the Incarnation can only be an act of Love (its

---

[52] See L. Polo, "La originalidad de la concepción cristiana de la existencia" (*Obras completas de Leonardo Polo*, v. XIII, Eunsa, Pamplona 2015, pp. 189 ff.)
[53] See 1 Jn 4:8
[54] See Phil 2:5-11

authorship is attributed to the Holy Spirit, whom the Church calls Gift, Love).

Thomas Aquinas, in the *Summa contra gentiles*, a work written to dialogue with Arabs and Jews, when trying to present the mystery of the Holy Trinity to them, says that all thinkers have glimpsed that God is wisdom, *logos*; what no one has suspected is the Holy Spirit, that is, that God is love[55]. That there is intelligence in God, that there is truth in God, all peoples have known, even though it may have only been vaguely (it is clear that Thomas Aquinas is referring to the peoples that he knew, especially those he directs his work to); but that in God there is will and love, this is only Christian.

Consequently, the Christian view of the will differs from the Greek view. As has been pointed out, Aristotle is aware of the existence of strictly possessive operations, which are superior to transitive and constructive actions, because since the latter are directed outwards, they imply a degree of possession that is weaker than the immanent operations. However, the immanent ones are cognitive operations. Neither in Aristotle nor in Plato (nor in any Greek thinker) is the will possessive; it is tendential, or rather, more precisely, non-possessive. It is also noteworthy that the Latin word *voluntas* has no Greek equivalent. What corresponds to what we call will is the word *orexis*, which means desire; in a more graphic sense, "wanting". Medical terminology uses the word "anorexic": lack of desire, lack of wanting. One tends to or desires that which one does not possess: one does not tend to that which is possessed. For this reason, the strictly perfect operation is the intellectual immanent operation, and by no means a tendency. Knowledge does not at all tend to what is known; there is no desiderative tension between thinking and what is thought. If one thinks, one has already thought what is thought; both are simultaneous.

Next to this, the will is (in Greek anthropology) what is imperfect. In man, as a being capable of possessing, it is pre-

---

[55] See Thomas Aquinas, *Summa contra gentiles*, I, 72 ff.

cisely the tendency that marks out the direction toward possession; but it does not in any way entail it. The being capable of having, considered according to its capacity, is not actual, but rather potential. And to this is likened the orectic. Inasmuch as man is a desiring being, insofar as he tends, he is an imperfect being. The imperfect in human nature is the will (and the lower tendencies)[56].

Certainly, the will is related to the intelligence. This is what Aristotle calls *boulesis* (and the medievals, *voluntas ut ratio*). It is equivalent to intention, purpose; the will is rational insofar as it is influenced by reason. In this way, desire is programmed and links to the means: it decides with regard to them. But there is no *boulesis* of the end[57]. This means that with respect to theory and to contemplation, the will is completely subordinated, since the possession of the end corresponds exclusively to the intellect. The will is "rationalized" in the medial pragmatic order: but the need for the means levels out human need. Thus, under no circumstances does the will cease being imperfect. Accordingly, there is no way that there can be a will in God.

In strictly pagan philosophy, that God loves—including that he loves himself—means that God is desire, desire of self. This is the Greek thesis expressed by Aristotle when he poses the problem of how the "unmoved mover" moves. For its part, the Platonic *eros* has the same connotation of imperfection: Eros is the son of Penia (poverty). Nevertheless, God is "pure act": He is having that is identical with itself, which, therefore, excludes this separation: the potentiality that desire introduces. One can desire God, but God, on the other hand, cannot. It is clear that if the will is only tendency and desire, then there is no place for it in God—a desiring God is a mythical notion or an aberrant gnostic illusion—, because it follows

---

[56] See L. Polo, *Antropología trascendental*, II. *La esencia de la persona humana*, Second Part (*Obras completas de Leonardo Polo*, v. XV, Eunsa, Pamplona 2016, pp. 367-530).

[57] See J. Aranguren, "Caracterización de la voluntad nativa", *Anuario Filosófico*, XXIX/2 (1996), pp. 347-358.

from this that God is imperfect: and an imperfect God is a contradiction.

The Aristotelian interpretation of the will is closely related to his definition of man. Longing is an imperfection because one longs only for that which one does not have. For an anthropology in which man is the being capable of having, not yet having or tending toward what one does not have is the imperfect dimension of man. And also the other way around: if the will is simply a human tendency, then the will never possesses. Possession is thereby exclusively cognitive. This is one of the reasons why the Stagirite insists on the importance of theory: in it, he discovers actual and sufficiently intimate possession. It is only from here that one can take the leap to the "pure act" of being. But, for this same reason, the perfection of the will is rejected.

Compared to this approach, Christian anthropology is an unsuspected novelty and, furthermore, an enormous opening up of horizons: it reinvigorates life and defines the meaning of history as a time moving forward. On the one hand, the distinction of love from desire requires transcending the idea of finality[58]. Briefly put, man's understanding is not just hyper-formal, but rather hyper-teleological. This is the contribution of Christian anthropology that is now being highlighted. Man certainly desires—it is a fact of experience—; the will certainly is a desiring faculty in man—not in God, but yes in man—. What is no longer true is that in man the will is only desirous.

Now, what could there be beyond the tendency to possess and possession itself? Obviously, giving, gifting. If the activity of the will is gifting, then it transcends that which the Greeks took as *telos*. Here we have Christian hyper-teleology.

---

[58] See J. M. Posada and I. García, "La índole intelectual de la voluntad y de lo voluntario en distinción con el amar" in Falgueras, Garcia, Padial (eds.), *Futurizar el presente. Estudios sobre la filosofía de Leonardo Polo*, Universidad de Málaga, Málaga 2003; pp.283-302; J. M. Posada, *Lo distintivo del amar*, Cuadernos de Anuario Filosófico, Serie Universitaria, 191, Servicio de Publicaciones de la Universidad de Navarra, Pamplona 2007; J. M. Posada *"Primalidades" de la amistad "de amor"*, Cuadernos de Anuario Filosófico, Serie Universitaria, 208, Servicio de Publicaciones de la Universidad de Navarra, Pamplona 2008.

Gifting is giving without losing, the activity that is superior to the equilibrium of losses and gains: gaining without acquiring or acquiring by giving[59].

The focal point of giving is of course found in Revelation. From a philosophical perspective, it is Augustine of Hippo who incorporated it into the cultural framework of the West and contributed to its literary expression (that is why he is called the father of Europe)[60]. To a great extent, we owe esteem for the truth, for the human capacity to know, to the Greeks; but we clearly owe the dimension of loving, elevated to the highest point, to Christianity.

Let us try to clarify some of the implications of this notion. Seen from its divine apex, the gift of love is operative. Thomas Aquinas understands creation as the gifting of being (*donatio essendi*): the creature is not a part of God (God does not have parts); it is bestowed reality. The bestowing is as radical as the reality[61]. For this reason, it is said that the creature is not presupposed: it is created from nothing (*ex nihilo*). Furthermore, it can be said that the bestowing of love gives human acting an "operating" character (the concept of operosity already refers to dynamic anthropology).

Christianity opens up perspectives that had been until then obscured or inaccessible. The only thing noble in man was his disinterested activity, that is, theory. The activities of the will were not disinterested; instead, they were tendential. And they remained either in the realm of useful tendencies or were directed towards knowledge. Their justification was centered on the integrity of the desired or practiced good. A further step was the voluntary disposition of what is had: letting go of it in favor of something else, even to the point of sacrifice. But in each and every case, having ruled over the voluntary act as its terminus or as what is offered (in this re-

---

[59] See R. Yepes, "Una nueva inspiración en la crisis de la antropología. Superar el tener con el dar", *Aceprensa*, Madrid 102/88 (1988) pp. 404-407.

[60] See J. A. Moreno, "Entender a San Agustín desde la filosofía poliana", *Studia Poliana*, 6 (2004), pp. 63-83.

[61] See J. A. García González, "Sobre el ser y la creación", *Anuario Filosófico*, XXIX/2 (1996), pp. 587-614.

gard we have the following saying: "no one can give what they do not have"). What I call the "operativity" of love is a type of generosity that decouples bestowing from having as a precondition, because by falling upon human actuation, it elevates it and gives to it something of it its very own character.

2.2 The person: giving as loving bestowal

But gifting also implies that human nature is now defined differently (and not in contradiction or in opposition to, nor even in concordance with Greek anthropology). Man is not ultimately defined—or solely defined—as the being capable of having, since it is necessary to find the root of his capacity for giving. The principle of gifting has to be more radical than immanence and even virtue. This is what is called intimacy[62]. The being capable of giving exists as a relationship to its origin, or, we could say, as "closer" than immanence. And this, strictly speaking, defines the notion of person[63]. Man is a personal being, because he is capable of giving. Seen from the person, giving means contributing: the contributing endorses the having. The notion of virtue too is taken up, and enters whole into the Christian vision of man. Greek anthropology is transcended by factors of greater radicality and scope. The person is what is most intimate, it is the very intimacy of man[64].

The opening up of intimacy implies the appearance in the world of that which never before existed in it because its origin is the person. This means that the person is above and

---

[62] See R. Yepes, "Persona: intimidad, don y libertad nativa. Hacia una antropología de los trascendentales personales", *Anuario Filosófico*, XXIX/2 (1996), pp. 1077-1104.

[63] See L. Polo, "La radicalidad de la persona" (*Obras completas de Leonardo Polo*, v. XIII, Eunsa, Pamplona 2015, pp. 85-99).

[64] "Person", for Polo does not mean the human "whole", that is, the body, its functions and faculties, plus the soul and its immaterial potencies, but rather that which is most radical in each man: the human act of being. See L. Polo *Antropología trascendental*, I. *La persona humana* (*Obras completas de Leonardo Polo*, v. XV, Eunsa, Pamplona 2016, pp. 21-278). Also see: S. Piá Tarazona, *El hombre como ser dual. Estudio de las dualidades radicales según la antropología trascendental de Polo*, Eunsa, Pamplona 1999; J. F. Sellés, *Antropología para inconformes*, Rialp, Madrid 2007.

beyond having. As origin of acts, it expands them to the extent that, being strictly a plus, it does not limit itself to initiating them, but rather continues in them. This installing himself into the acts that he originates is what makes it possible to say that man is the ex-sistent. The person adds and is added, or, what is the same, bestows operatively. This (which is something more than interest, but which also surpasses disinterest) can be designated by the Augustinian expression *ordo amoris*.

For the Greeks, man is a natural, living being, that is distinguished or is defined by the capacity for having. Seen from this deeper, new perspective, which corresponds to a greater openness, it must be stated that man is distinguished from physical entities to a degree much greater than the Greeks thought: he is distinguishes as a person, as standing beyond the world (astral, as well as sublunar). As a person, man is a second creature that is added to the world, since the person is not a specific difference—it is not correct to say that man is a personal animal—.

Consequently, the Greek definition of man is not denied; something is added to it that does not form part of that definition, but rather transcends and sustains it. Man's possessive capacity is, ultimately, sanctioned, ratified; but it is, moreover, sustained by a strictly radical instance that keeps it from being detained in possession, from ending in itself: it is projected or opens up, so to speak, as a vector of transcendence.

2.3 Free destining

Kant maintained that anthropology consists of the answer to the questions: What am I capable of knowing? What must I do? and What am I allowed to hope in? Now, the answer to the first two, which comes from Greece, is, I insist, at its core, correct: Kant does not add anything of note. The third question, which is an expansion of the previous ones, must be replaced by this other: What does human hope, as Christianity formulates it, mean? That is, what is hope in the order of love? The question can also be expressed like this: what is my life's task? or what is my life as task? The task is an expansion of freedom from personal intimacy. For the Greeks, freedom is dominion over acts insofar as they follow the means-ends relationship. But there must be a freedom in the hope-filled task inserted within the loving bestowal[65].

Thus, by establishing that having is continued and endorsed in the form of gifting, we discover a notion that goes beyond that of an end, and which I will call destining[66]. That destining is beyond the end becomes clear if man is not simply a being that is distinct from other entities because of his capacity for possessing an end, but rather because he is second creature: because then my end is not the world nor even God as author of the world, but rather God as my creator—creator of the person that I am—and as a person with a human nature by becoming incarnate.

Accordingly, for the Christian, hoping does not mean waiting. The question of hope does not refer to what will come about. Kant's question, "What am I allowed to hope in?", does not mean that I travel up to a terminus the coming about and the content of which needs to be discovered. If the meaning of my life is not limited to happiness according to the Greek understanding, that is, to a perfect possession; if instead my activity redounds in giving from the person, then destining is not to be confused with destiny. The question of destining lies in the one who it is destined to. To say it in some way, when taking stock of all that is from the person, man finds that this is not enough but rather that he must find a terminus that is not the terminus of desire, but rather of offering.

An attempt will be made to express this difficult question in a more graphic way. It is not primarily a question of attaining high goals, but of giving. But then, who is going to accept it? The field of resonance of my capacity for giving must also be personal. Otherwise this capacity is absurd. The German

---

[65] See L. Polo, *Persona y libertad* (*Obras completas de Leonardo Polo*, v. XIX, Eunsa, Pamplona 2017).
[66] See R. Corazón, "Eudaimonía y destino", *Studia Poliana*, 2 (2000), pp. 165-189; I. Falgueras, *Hombre y destino*, Eunsa, Pamplona 1998.

poet Rilke takes this question up when he writes: "Who among the angels will hear my cry?", or rather, "Who responds to my hope-filled initiative?". The fundamental problem is correspondence. Thomas Aquinas states it clearly: absolutely speaking, without correspondence, love does not exist[67]. With regard to this point, there is no room for the unilateralism that desiring a paradigm implies—desire is not absolute—. Without correspondence, the superiority of gifting love with respect to desire would make no sense. Hope is based on loving reciprocity and is directed to fostering it above human velleities: man is authorized to hope for it. Hope is not a tendency, because it is based on love and seeks to correspond.

With this, the theme of Christian hope has been presented in a general way. It is the search for acceptance and for response; that is, the hope of encountering a likeness. Here, "likeness" does not mean copy or reiteration, but rather alterity of initiatives in replica, which draws them together and places them on the same level. For this reason, the notion of "neighbor" is one of the fundamental categories of Christian sociology. This notion means that if I am a being capable of loving, then the other has to be such that he not be inferior to me or deprived of that capacity.

From this comes the notion that all men are equal. Equality[68] among men is not only of the species, but is found in their personal dignity. But it is, furthermore, a requirement of Christian life. If the others are not equal to me, then what does it mean that I give to them?: to whom do I give? These questions do not, in the first place, refer to reception nor, therefore, to the receptive capacity. A neighbor is not the destination of gifting solely as a receptor. Gifting looks first of all to dignification, and excludes the possibility that the others

---

[67] See Thomas Aquinas, *Summa contra gentiles*, Bk. I, ch. 100. Regarding this, see: J. A. Lombo, "Lo trascendental antropológico en Tomás de Aquino. Las raíces clásicas de la propuesta de Leonardo Polo", *Studia Poliana*, 6 (2004), pp. 181-208.

[68] Equality is little for or from the person. It can be said: yes, no man is—as person—less than another; but since person is being-more, this declaration does not preclude the distinction: each person is distinct, not equal.

might not be capable of being dignified. It is this that regulates the content of the gift.

It thus becomes clear that hope is not structurally desire, but rather a powerful requirement that is doubly directed, above and beyond adaptation or equilibrium. Hope is not homeostatic since it seeks and promotes the dignity of all men. From this arises an imperative that—modifying a Kantian phrase—can be expressed like this: do not be satisfied with the means. This non-conformity with what has been done is dissatisfaction: it is not a tendency, but a refusal to stop, to say: "enough". This too is Augustinian.

Dissatisfaction is equivalent to not getting tired of giving. It therefore does not involve a negative attitude; but it does bring with it a letting-be. This letting-be can in many cases be described (in others it implies a renunciation) as a sharing and a collaborating, which breaks through the limits of having. What we usually call "interpersonal communication" lies in the correlative flexibility of the distinction between what is mine and what is yours.

If one looks carefully, this flexibility appears in immanent possession, although still in a unilateral way. Understanding a thing is already a kind of gifting: the thing is not less than itself when it is being understood; and since it is incapable of understanding itself, being understood is conferred upon it. This adequation is, however, unsatisfactory when seen in terms of the promotion of human dignity that hope seeks and with regard to which it is availed-of as a task. For this reason, hope does not claim authorship of the bestowal, nor does it demand its recognition: it renounces any attention given to it, precisely because it does not renounce giving, and because dissatisfaction is equivalent to not getting tired of giving.

A capacity for loving that is completely solitary would be absolute tragedy. This is how the tragic dimension of Christian anthropology comes to be formulated. If others cannot be dignified, then I am a being without meaning; I have, so to say, an excessively large charge that I cannot discharge into anything: I have a capacity that is nullified at its terminus. Because the terminus of hope is not what is one's own, but the other.

2.4 Intimacy

It has so far been pointed out that Western anthropology draws from two sources. A mature formulation of the Greek source is found in Aristotle. The second is the Christian contribution, which—while taking account of the maturity of the Aristotelian approach—was framed as a modification of the meaning of the will. For the Christian, the will is a divine attribute. And this means that it is a sign of perfection, not only of something lacking. For an anthropology that, like that of the Greeks, defines man by having in act, the will is integrated in the form of a tendency to possess, something which interferes with the notion of divine will and gives rise to an impassive and impersonal God. The Greek philosophers speak of the divine, (not of the personal God).

For its part, divine love is the only possible reason for the Incarnation. Accordingly, the will is a faculty that is much higher than that which the Greeks dared to think. Love is an initiative; it is not a pure awakening to what is desirable, but rather it has an intimate source. Love leads to discovering the "personal" character of man. Christian anthropology is "personalist". Nor is the notion of "person" found in the classical Greek thinkers; it is one of the omissions of that anthropology, which is, on the other hand, so insightful within its own limits.

For personalist humanism, man not only possesses in a more or less intense form, but rather—as they say in Italy—*fá di se*, (gives of himself). Man is an innovating being, on whose activities depends something that would in no way exist without it. He is innovating because he contributes; and not from the world, but from himself. Man is characterized, above all, by intimacy. Intimacy is one of the marks of the person. Intimacy is not being closed, or a being locked inside, but rather a relationship of origin. Person means relationship of origin or, said in another way, it establishes an originating reference in what it contributes: a not desisting from it; something like a seal, an endorsement. That which proceeds from the person is not impersonal but rather is guaranteed as authentic. Task and sending are notions that are correlative with that of authenticity.

It must, nevertheless, be said that the notion of virtue—one of the great acquisitions of the classical consideration of man—implies hyperformalization; that is, the optimized and intrinsic restructuring of human nature: the achievement of new points of departure, the disruption of the lineal approach, of the determinism of initial conditions: the exercise of freedom with respect to the means. However, the growth in the understanding of man that Christianity introduces goes from hyperformalization to hyperfinalization.

As a being that gives of itself, man proposes goals for himself that are higher than those that the means-end or tendency-objective relationship allows. The meaning of the Greek *telos* is situated within nature. In contrast, hyperteleology arises from the person. This *plus* of finality is usually approached with the concept of the supernatural, which belongs to Theology. Here it has been called destination, (not destiny). Man's activity can be destined—it is given—, and requires someone to whom it is destined. The structure of love, insofar as it is a perfect act, implies a response: someone who is at the same level as the gifting, someone for whom the gifting is not just received. The gifting is not mere beneficence, but rather implies a dignifying intention that is focused on the idea of neighbor.

The equality of all men takes its highest sense from the notion of neighbor. Separated from it, it can fall under the influence of resentment or of envy. This mistaken connotation, which transforms equality into a more or less altered or damaged echo, can perhaps be perceived in the French Revolution's motto—*liberté, egalité, fraternité*—considered, at least, in its historical application. An equality between isolated individuals, or among individuals unified by a totalitarian convocation, is an oscillating concept, the fruit of an inspiration that only weakly reflects its point of departure.

The idea of neighbor is clearly reversible. If I am capable of gift, then gift implies a justification on the part of the one it is destined to. But it is also true that if the dignity of the one who it is destined to is assured beforehand, then my capacity for giving is put to the test. On the other hand, human gifting, considered absolutely, is not primary, but is preceded by divine gifting. The discussion of this key question explains the variations that have been introduced into anthropology in the modern age.

2.5 Reason's offering and faith

Certain currents of modern thought have wavered with respect to whom it is that the human possibility of offering is ultimately destined. If the one to whom human offering is destined is not God, then an internal limitation in the gifting tension is produced that has repercussions for the appreciation of human dignity. For this reason, atheism—as a phase of certain ideological currents whose point of departure is Christian—brings with it a curious problem: that of inventing for itself the one to whom action is destined, the one who justifies the offertive creative capacity that man bestows. This problem is puzzling because its solution is impossible. For this reason, it unfolds along a double reduction: it ends in anthropological pessimism and in a strange identification of the giver with the one to whom it is destined[69]. Most notably, the gift value of the intelligence is cast into doubt.

---

[69] Among these philosophies is that of Marx, Nietzsche, Freud, etc. See: L. Polo, *Nietzsche como pensador de dualidades* (*Obras completas de Leonardo Polo*, v. XVII, Eunsa, Pamplona 2018). Also: J. F. Sellés, "¿Es el hombre un eventual viajero, o un ser eternizable? Nietzsche a debate en Polo", *Studia Poliana*, 8 (2006), pp. 269-286. With regard to this topic in Marx, in addition to the earlier mentioned work by Polo (*La antropología de Marx*), the author also has another unpublished work: *Aspectos fundamentales del pensamiento de Marx*. With regard to Freud, see C. Martínez Priego, "Freud y Polo. La superación poliana de la propuesta psicoanalítica", *Studia Poliana*, 7 (2005), pp. 119-142.

In fact, the great tension that the existential realization of this anthropology implies, which is directed by the historical influence of Christianity, is not reduced to voluntary activity, but rather extends to intellectual activity. This is seen, for example, in the interpretation of philosophy. The formulation of philosophy from the Catholic view consists in intellectual activity's value as an offering. In this sense, philosophy acquires the character of being a servant to faith. Faith, as consistency of what is hoped for, brings the intelligence and the will together in accordance with their gift meaning. Reason is contributed[70]. The Christian view is the only one that calls for a theology. No other religious reality elevates man's intellectual capacity to such a level. Theology is the most amazing and far reaching intellectual accomplishment in history, and is carried out with the reason's sense of offering[71]. Reason finds its own destination in the clarification of dogmatic mystery; it puts itself to the test inasmuch as it is capable of contributing its light to that which primarily, and without ever ceasing to be so in this life, is mystery.

Now, adhering to faith without reason's offering is fideism. Fideism is a formulation of the peculiar problem that was alluded to earlier: man is incapable of gifting his mind to God. At the same time, the dogmatic mystery becomes an insoluble problem. The so-called divorce of faith and reason begins here. Fideism is a modality of despair. Starting from there, thought concerns itself with other things (or seeks to take control of faith. This is what happens in the peculiar Gnosticism that is German idealism).

In any case, the fideist vacillation does not completely ruin the gifting openness that man finds within himself when his capacity for wanting is established. This openness is concen-

---

[70] On this topic see Polo's "Itinerario de la razón hacia la fe" (*Obras completas de Leonardo Polo*, v. XXVII, Eunsa, Pamplona 2017, pp. 70-76), inspired by a work of I. Falgueras.

[71] On the topic of theology, see Polo's "Saberes humanos y revelación cristiana" (*Obras completas de Leonardo Polo*, v. XXVII, Eunsa, Pamplona 2017, pp. 35-62). Also see: A. Bayer, "La 'fides qua creditur' como elevación del conocer personal según la antropología trascendental de Leonardo polo", *Studia Poliana*, 9 (2007), pp. 191-214.

trated in the concept of hope[72]. Christianity has brought hope to the table and has incorporated it into history in a very definite manner. Hope has caught the attention of men who have come to realize what the Christian influence means existentially. Péguy for example, compares hope to a reed cane: it is the flexibility of our journeying.

3. Hoping

We will now attempt, first of all, an analysis of hope's task. Second, the modern crises of hope: that is, some of the vicissitudes of anthropology in the Modern Age will be described. Ever since Christianity has had an influence in history, in culture, and in education, hope presents itself as that axis which gives meaning and tempers our life. It is the firm and, at the same time, elastic framework of our existence; the redoubled interest that directs the plexus of practice toward the dignity of the person.

3.1 Optimism

The first element of hope is optimism. Hope carries within it optimism; and also, conversely, the only legitimate optimism is one that dwells within hope. Pessimism encloses and paralyzes. In contrast, the hope-filled man directs himself to what is best, comes out of self-absorption and puts himself into the task; he goes out of himself, he ex-sists, precisely because his contribution prolongs his intimacy. On the other hand, an optimism without hope is trivial and estranged[73]. Optimism in the face of the present situation is superficial and precarious: it is the optimism of someone who has made it; not of someone who is in the task or in the destination, but

---

[72] The concept of *hope* in L. Polo has a similar meaning to that of St. Gregory of Nyssa.

[73] A short work by Polo related with this theme is "El optimismo ante la vida" (*Obras completas de Leonardo Polo*, v. XVI, Eunsa, Pamplona 2018, pp. 37-44).

rather of one who is satisfied: an optimism empty of promises, alienated in what is inert. As I said, the satisfied person is someone who thinks that what he has done is enough (*satisfacere*) and, therefore, disregards improvement and the novelty of contribution. He thus wallows in retention, in recuperation. This is the intimately tired man who, for example, lies beneath Feuerbach's anthropology.

The optimism of hope is therefore dissatisfied. Hope implies dissatisfaction, and therein lies its peculiar optimism, which is the authentic one. A satisfied optimism is as ridiculous as resting on one's laurels, and since it is not followed by anything better, it withers away. We have certainly all have had the experience of striving toward a goal. Once attained, anyone who attempts to settle down in it immediately notices a reluctance, a certain unpleasantness. The optimism of the man who lives in hope is dissatisfied because he is never reduced to the present.

For this reason, what is normally called "secularized hope" is an abdication, because the consummation of hope does not belong to this world. There is an British saying that can help to make this clear: "the optimist is someone who says that we are in the best of all possible worlds; the pessimist is someone who believes that this is true." This optimistic pessimism, or pessimistic optimism, that is reflected in this paradox (which is a bit tongue in cheek), is foreign to hope, which flat out rejects the idea of the Leibnizian best of all possible worlds[74]: in that world there is nothing left to do. That is, within it nothing better is possible; it is closed to human endeavors: it is a world for those who have retired from existing. In the best of all possible worlds, it is not possible to hope.

Hope is thus formed from an optimism that refers to the future. It includes putting oneself on the line: leaving the present situation in search of another. In sum, the person who lives in hope affirms that we are in a world that can be im-

---

[74] Regarding this point: Mª S. Fernández García, "Leibniz y Polo", *Studia Poliana*, 7 (2005), pp. 173-184; "La necesidad como totalidad de la posibilidad en Leibniz", *Anuario Filosófico*, XXIX/2 (1996), pp. 527-537.

proved. That is why she does not settle down in the present, but lives or exists precisely in the trajectory that leads to what is better. Without hope, it would not be possible to exist, because existing means both going out and being in the going out. Only she who does not have the mentality of settling down in the now "ex-sists". Existing and being in hope are the same. Sistere-extra, to be in the going out, implies, precisely, abandoning immobility.

Aristotle said something in this regard. For him, the most imperfect is what is immobile, when it means the lack of hope for an act. For this reason, according to Aristotle, the most imperfect is the center of the Earth. This is a consequence of Aristotle's geocentricism, a thesis that is often misunderstood. What is lowest, where there is no hope or from where one cannot get out, is the tomb: the subterranean, the infernal.

This observation concerning the Greek mind makes a brief psychological analysis of the lived experience of hope possible. Hope is dissatisfied. This is not, however, the same as the "orectic" tendency of the Greeks, which is lived from need; something has to be done; one must act, because otherwise one dies of hunger. On the other hand, not considering what one has as sufficient because one is aspiring to better things is a different situation. Dissatisfaction is restlessness, but not uneasiness or agitation. Hegel maintains that the soul of the dialectic process is the lack of peace. He is mistaken, and it is not just a question of nuance. Aiming for more, insofar as giving, is superior to having. Which does not mean that having is of little value or is bad. Aiming for more is not running away either—that is where the *phygé* that the last Greeks spoke of is—: it is not flight from an inhospitable world in which it is not possible to live. Hope is dissatisfied not because the situation is bad, but because something better is wanted.

Even without insisting on the lived experiences that accompany hope—and this analysis is not what is most important either—, it can still be pointed out that hope is not revolutionary. Nor is dissatisfaction an insult directed at the present situation. To justify leaving by insulting the present is very much mistaken. Psychologically, this is discovered right away. This is, unfortunately, at the core of one part of liberation theology[75].

But if revolution is a false version of hope, conformism is also contrary to it[76]. The conformist remains stuck in the situation[77], not so much because he considers it good, but because he thinks that he cannot get out of it. This is the man who says: "it is what it is; come what may, and it can't be done because it can't be done." As forms of referring to the situation in order to justify not moving, these tautological expressions seem to be a good characterization of the conformist, who does not live in hope, but rather in conformism: "it is what it is". What else is there? Nothing. Who is in charge? Money, the party, immediate gratifications rule. Things are simply the way they are; they cannot be changed. Why can't they? Because they cannot. This last explicative tautology of giving up is perhaps what is most characteristic of conformism.

3.2 The future and the task

Now, if the first ingredient of hope is optimism, the second—in agreement with what we have been saying—is the future. If there is no future—that is, if we turn our back on the task—, then hope cannot be established. Better said, it can be established in a false way, namely, by making it atemporal; by placing what is hoped for at an ending that will come about by virtue of a fatal dynamic, that is to say, something outside of human undertakings. This falsified hope (falsified by its being emptied of human bestowal, of man's gifting activity) is precisely what is called utopia. The utopian man speaks like this: "times are bad: there is nothing that can be done (in this

---

[75] With regard to this topic, see L. Polo, "La teología de la liberación y el futuro de América" (*Obras completas de Leonardo Polo*, v. XIII, Eunsa, Pamplona 2015, pp. 189-253).

[76] It is in this sense that the following work is to be understood: J. F. Sellés, *Antropología para inconformes*, Madrid, Rialp, 2nd ed., 2007.

[77] A more extensive presentation by Polo of the current situation is given in the introduction to *Antropología de la acción directiva* (*Obras completas de Leonardo Polo*, v. XVIII, Eunsa, Pamplona 2019, pp. 311-312).

he says the same thing as the conformist), but something better will come about". How will it come about? Well, it will come about without me intervening, without counting on me. Clearly, although it is postponed, the pessimistic optimism of the British saying is thereby repeated. Utopia accepts that we are not in the best of all possible worlds, but we will be. Now, this will happen automatically, following the fatality of extra-human forces[78].

That is a falsification of hope, not only because that future will not come about, but because by being extraneous to human contribution, it cannot be better nor, indeed, human. Utopia is the dehumanization of hope. Utopians are almost as numerous as conformists. The ideologies that we spoke of on other occasions[79], which attribute the passage from zero-sum games to positive sum ones to the invisible hand or to the dialectic, are utopian. Evolutionism too has a utopian tendency.

If hope is inserted into the transition toward the future; that is, if the best is yet to come and will not arrive without counting on me; if hope is incompatible with utopia, then the best for me is a task with a twofold sense. The task is the third element of hope. This task involves me intimately and, consequently, takes on the character of a duty: I have to improve. Hope proposes a future to me; but, unlike utopia, I will be this future if I make myself better. Hope involves me intrinsically: if I move towards what is better, then I have to be better. The invariability of the subject is the pessimism of utopia: a mediocre man in a magnificent world. The Gospel parable that speaks of the wedding guest who lacks a wedding garment is a portrait of utopia.

3.3 Risk

The fourth element of hope appears here. If I am not an enthusiast of utopia; if for me the future is a task and some-

---

[78] This is the style, according to Polo of A. Smith's economic utopia of the invisible hand and of Marxist dialectic.

[79] Liberalism, communism, and social democracy.

thing that will not come about without me, then I have to ask myself about what resources I can count upon to undertake this task. This is the corner stone of the idea of business.

When it comes to the task of hope, the question concerning resources is rather complex. First of all, it is clear that for someone who considers himself completely miserable, who is good for nothing, the question arises: what is he going to hope for? He can hope that something happens; but with what does he contribute? Obviously, some resources are needed. But it is also clear that one cannot count on all of them. Otherwise, if all the resources necessary for reaching a better future already exist, then that future is the present and requires no task at all. Thus, the future that one seeks cannot be completely certain. Hope therefore implies risk. And it is good that it implies it, because without risk there is no place for novelty. And risk is, moreover, the guarantee that is specific to giving, that is, that having is not what is highest.

If all the resources necessary for carrying out a project can be counted upon, then it is best not to go through with it, because it will not bring about anything new, nor will it improve the agent. Certainly, there would be no obligation to propose it. But it should be noted that this situation is unreal. First, because if I can already count on everything that I need to make a contribution and if I stick to that, then I am not making a contribution; instead, I am limiting myself to having (although this sufficiency is not general). Second, because what proceeds from the actual sufficient resources is enjoyment. However, although it is legitimate, enjoyment (*frui*) is not the supreme act of the will[80], for which reason hope does not look solely to this act (the supreme act of the will is the one that follows upon contemplation: singing glory). There is a Gospel parable for this case too: that man who had a large harvest, and judged replanting to be useless. This man, says the Lord, was a fool.

---

[80] The exposition of the acts of the will by Polo can be found in the second part of *Antropología trascendental*, II (*Obras completas de Leonardo Polo*, v. XV, Eunsa, Pamplona 2016, pp. 367-530).

Consequently, hope cannot be relinquished; and the future is better than the present. But insofar as it depends on me, it is only possible, not certain: the resources that I avail of today are not sufficient. The hypothesis of counting upon all that is necessary for the task insofar as it depends on me is contradictory. Today's resources are always scarce with respect to hope. It is here where risk appears. Whoever wants to avoid the risk of human life eliminates hope.

Risk is one of the aspects of life in which love's generosity is better seen. Why does one take a risk? Because one gives; even more, because one accepts giving under conditions of insufficiency: in hope and not in fullness. On the other hand, taking cover under guarantees, demanding assurances, is a form of timidity or of spiteful arrogance: another modality of the utopia that seeks the automation of processes; or the worry of an old man.

3.4 Convoking help

Risk is also what unites, because if one contributes all the necessary resources he does not count on others, he does not seek help. But help is the community of hope, its extension and, therefore, a requirement. A hope that refuses to be shared is contradictory: individualist, not personal.

Furthermore, only those who step forward, assuming the risk, have the capacity for convocation and can be guides. When the problem of ruling minorities (that is, of groups that mark out the historical destination of a human society) is posed, the first thing that should be asked is how much risk they are ready to assume. If they are constantly seeking assurances and become unnerved or give up when faced with risk, then it must be said that that society does not have a ruling minority and that it lacks unity.

Without an open and convoking hope, distrust appears. One assumes risk because one trusts, that is, because the task of personal dignification belongs to the realm of man's creative design. Otherwise, risk is irrational and foreign to hope.

The only attractive project is one that convokes. To convoke is to declare both that one cannot do it alone, as well as that isolated triumph is not what matters. Accepting the convocation is not the same as signing up for or joining the winning party. Hope is not one-sided in this sense. Moreover, the one who convokes admits that she does not exclude failure and that she hopes in others. Her merit lies in putting herself forward. Therefore, if she perhaps fails, it is a sign that it is something serious, in such a way that if we exclude this possibility we are reducing the project's scope. This is the well-known advice of the frightened mother to her pilot son: "my son, fly low and slow". This does not seem to be good advice. On the one hand, because that way of flying increases the likelihood of crashing. On the other hand, because flying slowly does not lead to the improvement of this means or to the discovery of other means of transport and, consequently, does not justify the aircraft. It must be said, at the expense of the mother, that she advises from the ground, without climbing on board: she does not fear for herself.

It is a mistake to think that more success is achieved when one acts with a hundred percent certainty. Those who take risks achieve higher goals. The others get left behind, and then later perhaps complain.

3.5 Revolutionaries and terrorists

It will be said that this approach justifies revolutionaries and terrorists. However, it seems to me that the revolutionary does not, strictly speaking, assume any risk, but rather does something different. Obviously, any man who attacks someone who opposes him risks death; but this is not the risk of hope, but rather a danger inherent to one's way of acting. If one attempts to topple an established system by force, and this system responds by shooting, then one is put at risk. I will make a few observations.

First. A terrorist is not the same as a revolutionary. The former does not count on the masses; they are their aggressors. The classical revolutionary (let us say, from around the 1930s) proclaims himself leader of the masses and functioned only insofar as the masses followed him. Mobilizing the masses: this is what the first communist revolutionaries, and even Hitler, sought. But this epoch has passed. Today revolutionaries are not mobilizers of the masses, but rather aggressors. Their project is destructive: a project against, not in favor of history. Nothing new is attempted, but rather a dismantling of what there is. And this is not hope at all, but rather the opposite of hope.

Second. It is destroying that is easier, not a task. Destroying is within anyone's reach. In the final analysis, it is the safest thing to do. On the other hand, one can fail when building. An artist takes risks: she may be right or wrong regarding her hope for making her idea a reality; but she will, nevertheless, never be satisfied.

Third. Hope is affirming; destruction, negative. Is it possible to affirm oneself as a person in what is negative? Kierkegaard makes a somewhat dramatic analysis of this point. The Dane, a keen observer of despair—the negative of hope—, defines the final degree like this: it is the despair of one who clings to his pessimistic vision of existence, identifying himself with it: if this identification is taken from him, he would then be left without a self. Consequently, despair reveals itself as contrary to hope on the very level of the person. The person, we were saying, bestows. This extreme despairer lacks an I to the point of having to procure one while falling into "diabolic madness": this is why he clings on to his tragedy, he identifies himself with negation in such a way that, if it is taken from him, he would think himself to be left without a self. This is how Kierkegaard describes the tragedy of the revolutionary (he writes around 1848). Certainly, few people live diabolical madness or radical despair. Kierkegaard constructs an interpretive model, not a portrait of a human type.

Fourth. The terrorist, I insist, is not the revolutionary of yesteryear, who was supported by a fervent mass of people: he counted on their support; he took considerable risks. But some thought that the best way to neutralize him was to get him to not take risks, or rather, to domesticate him. In one way or another, the task of domesticating the old romantic revolutionaries has been accomplished, although not without giving rise to ridiculous or sad episodes, depending on how one views it.

It has already been pointed out that risk produces commitments. We Spaniards were rather romantic in the 1920s and 30s. However, even then those attempts at domestication produced results, as reflected in a brief story about revolutionaries who travelled by train to lead a rally in a city. In those times there were cars of first, second, and third class; today third class has been eliminated because they are bothersome and uncomfortable: wooden seats for people with little money. That is where the revolutionaries naturally should have gone. They were, however, traveling in first class, but shortly before arriving at their destination they moved to third class. They thereby ran very grave risks of destroying the hopes that had been raised. Here we have an enormous responsibility: if one fails because of hypocrisy, it causes demoralization. A people betrayed by long-established leaders who call themselves revolutionaries is a people of cynics, says Sakharov[81].

With this, some features of hope have been sketched out. However, it must be added that man is not only author or co-author of the future, but that he is also constituted by his past. In this sense he takes up something that he did not contribute to making. Nevertheless, the reception of tradition is also re-creation, especially if the tradition includes hope. Here it would be appropriate, and very interesting, to study tradition, because it is also an aspect of great importance in Christian anthropology. But it is not possible to cover all the themes. It would be good to continue along the path of hope.

---

[81] See L. Polo, "Revolución es sustituir una clase dirigente por otra" (*Obras completas de Leonardo Polo*, v. XVI, Eunsa, Pamplona 2018, pp. 131-137).

3.6 Voluntarism and nihilism in modern philosophy

Having established the main features of hope, it is now time to examine its alternations or fluctuations in modern anthropology. I will first propose a brief outline of modern thought that begins much earlier than normally thought. It is ordinarily said that the first modern philosopher is Descartes or, during the same time period, Bacon. But it is more accurate to argue that the first moderns are the voluntarist nominalists of the 14th century[82].

The Modern Era begins with the inversion of the relative importance of the will and the intelligence. For the Greeks, what is perfect is thinking; the will is imperfect, since it is not a principle of possessive acts. Overcoming this disparity is a Christian contribution. Love is a perfect act and is accompanied by an entourage of acts that are also perfect—the description of which would be lengthy—[83].

The beginning of the Modern Age is the change of the Greek disparity: intelligence, knowledge, is now what is imperfect in man. This is voluntarism[84]. Modernity is born with the thesis that the will is spontaneous and independent of the intelligence; therefore, it functions as an arbitrary force[85]. If the will is triggered by itself without waiting for reason, then it is the will that is dominant, and the intelligence is passive. The intelligence, like a mirror, reflects the world; it is not what is active in man. Consequently, what is thought as a reflection of the world is the possibility of the world, not its reality (something that corresponds to the will).

---

[82] See L. Polo, *Nominalismo, idealismo y realismo* (*Obras completas de Leonardo Polo*, v. XIV, Eunsa, Pamplona 2016). Also see: F. Domínguez – J. F. Sellés, "Nominalismo, voluntarismo y contingentismo. La crítica de Leonardo Polo a las nociones centrales de Ockham", *Studia Poliana*, 9, (2007), pp. 155-190.

[83] See the aforementioned publication by Polo, *Antropología trascendental*, II, Second Part (*Obras completas de Leonardo Polo*, v. XV, Eunsa, Pamplona 2016, pp. 367-530).

[84] See J. A. García, "La voluntad y el voluntarismo en gnoseología según los escritos del profesor Polo", *Studium*, 25 (1985), pp. 515-522.

[85] See J. A. García, "Polo frente a Escoto: libertad o voluntad", *Studia Poliana*, 9 (2007), pp. 47-65.

This one-sided vindication of the will is clearly dependent on the Christian discovery of the person. But it is also clear that it weakens it: spontaneity is not a contribution. There is a shift from personalism to subjective individualism. The idea that man is driven by a blind and uncooperative inner force has yielded extremely bitter fruits. The one who clearly perceived this was a very sincere thinker who followed the trajectory of voluntarism to the end: Frederick Nietzsche.

Indeed, the thinker from Röcken observes that a will posited as what first in the man is productive over and beyond the human subject. This is the idea of the superman. "Superman" means that a primary will cannot be anything but the will to will or is forced into self-reference[86]. This self-reference of the will is what Nietzsche calls the will to power[87].

But the destiny of a dynamic self-reference is a future that is closed in on itself, that is, a future that does not mark out any direction. Nietzsche calls this overcoming. Overcoming implies that with regard to the will to power, the definitive as exterior to it does not exist: that would be the past. Insofar as the past is not what is definitive external to the will, time is curved. This is what Nietzsche calls the eternal recurrence of the same[88].

Nietzsche warns that voluntarism is not compatible with hope. This is what one of his aphorisms says: the will to power is forever nothingness (*Der wille zur Macht und nichts ausserdem*)[89]. Nothingness appears when the will functions in a regime of

---

[86] See J. F. Sellés, "¿Es curva la voluntad? Acotaciones sobre la hermenéutica nietzscheana", *Studia Poliana*, 7 (2005), pp. 241-249.

[87] "this mystery world of the twofold voluptuous delight, my 'beyond good and evil,' without goal, unless the joy of the circle is itself a goal; without will, unless a ring feels good will toward itself— do you want a name for this world? A solution for all of its riddles? A light for you, too, you best-concealed, strongest, most intrepid, most midnightly men?— This world is the will to power—and nothing besides! And you yourselves are also this will to power—and nothing besides!" (*The Will to Power*, fr. 1067 from 1885. Translated by Anthony M. Ludovici, 1913).

[88] See the aforementioned book by Polo: *Nietzsche como pensador de dualidades*, cap. V: Vida, voluntad de poder, eterno retorno y superhombre (*Obras completas de Leonardo Polo*, v. XVII, Eunsa, Pamplona 2018, pp. 137-157).

[89] See F. Nietzsche, *N.*, 7 (54), 1886-1887, *KSA* 12, 312-313.

isolation and of sovereignty; in other words, when the classical dimension of Western culture is denied. Voluntarism confuses wanting with being, it dissolves being into wanting-to-be. This destroys the unity of the person: it leads to its becoming disturbed, as Kierkegaard noted.

For his part, Nietzsche realizes that a self-referring will, with which the I finds itself forced to merge, a will that self-gives itself, that seeks to reclaim its own gifting character for itself, is confused with the need for self-production. For this reason, Nietzsche speaks of the metaphysics of the artist. But self-production neutralizes the gift: it reduces it to filling an absence. In this misguided contortion of human bestowing, the gifting intimately decays, and thus nothingness comes about in the will.

The naked will, at the summit and in its own solitude, suggests the solitude of the sun. Nietzsche says that every sun is cold with respect to another sun. Ultimately, Nietzsche, like Kierkegaard, finds himself facing nothingness. With the nothingness of what? With the nothingness of the other. This altered will lacks an other; that is, it is its own other and, therefore, neither loves nor hopes. Hope sketches out nothingness, if it is gifting without beneficiary, "with" self-beneficiary.

Now, the nihilism of hope is not exactly hedonism because it also nullifies pleasure. It is not mere recovery. Feuerbach is an insignificant voluntarist when compared to Nietzsche. Nietzsche sees, beyond, the empty depths of a recovering subjectivity, and the nothingness of a productive will taken as a protective redoubt of the subject. The madness begins when one discovers that the will must nevertheless make way for the other. This explosion is very well described in the passages of book III of *Zarathustra* that suggest that the divinity is inevitable.

Nietzsche walks the path of voluntarism to the end. A will without a superior, that is supra-personal, that does not even have an equal, perceives the other only as an overcoming of itself. But this overcoming implies weakness: it is the confirmation of one's own strength which, as Nietzsche says, can only be done with scales and columns. That is why destiny appears precisely as nothingness.

Furthermore, the notion of nothingness is another Christian discovery. The Greeks never spoke of nothingness; they spoke of non-being, which is something else. Nothingness goes together with the notion of creation, as has already been pointed out: God creates out of nothing (*ex nihilo*). At the same time, nothingness is also discovered in the attempt to explore man's solitary will. While the nothingness of creation is, so to speak, initial, Nietzsche's nothingness is terminal. And this can be explained because God creates—he creates the other: he creates out of love—; in contrast, the will in production is the overcoming that avoids its own weakness: it is completely curved and does not create—it does not create the other—. This absence of the other is terminal nothingness, which dwells as intimate contradiction within the will to power.

Nietzsche is only possible from Christianity: as a tragic experience of creation in reverse. A will as a project for improving seems like a hope-filled project; but it is an improvement that is exclusively for itself, as will to will. Thus, it closes itself off from every destination within the very project of destiny itself. "Nothingness forever" is a comment on the attempt against hope, on what happens when one refuses to love.

3.7 *The nothingness of the other as love of self*

Thomas Aquinas too perceives the curvature of the will. The will is curved insofar as it refers to itself in order to love more, but not insofar as it refers to the other. And without reference to the other there is neither hope nor love. For this reason, if the curvature of the will closes in unto itself in pure reference to itself, then the will to will, or for the will, appears: the will to power; ultimately, the inability to love. Amorous impotence is nothingness.

The discovery of nothingness does not strictly speaking belong to the intelligence. The intelligence can think non-being in comparison with being, but it cannot think nothingness (this would be equivalent to not thinking). Nothingness is not a hole—it is not to be confused with the void, imprecision, or indeterminacy—; nothingness is precisely thinking the will without intention of the other[90]. The discovery of nothingness belongs to the intelligence when it turns to the paralysis of the will. Nothingness as pure absence is a fortified will that wants to gather into itself: it refuses adhesion and severs its connection to the other. This rupture nullifies the wanting at its emerging from its projection. The absence of the other has repercussions backwards. Tragic nothingness thus takes place within the very heart of the voluntary act.

Nietzsche is a great witness to what happens if what can be called "sacrilegious robbery" takes place; that is, if what is most contrary to Christianity takes place: its cultural utilization in solipsist, selfish terms. The corruption of the best is the worst. There are versions of Christian culture that are almost abysmal in their perversity. If this line is carried forward with Nietzsche's inflexibility, then what it is hiding is discovered. It is usually said that Nietzsche is the philosopher of unmasking. Lou Andrea Salomé, who knew him well, and who was also a disciple of Freud, took note of the difference between voluntarist inquiry and the spontaneity of Freudian instinct. Psychoanalytic unmasking is not very deep.

Unmasking. What happens when someone, effectively reinforced in their endowment of will, wants it for themselves? Nothing at all. That is, nothingness takes place. Tragedy as nothingness appears on man's horizon with surprising clarity when beyond desire (Nietzsche frequently longs for the weakness of desire) a new impulse is destroyed in its confrontation with eternity. Returning to Rilke: no one listens to him.

---

[90] The intentionality of the will is that of *alterity*, and belongs to its acts of wanting, while that of the intelligence is of *likeness*, and belongs to objects of thought. This is a basic point in medieval philosophy. See the aforementioned book by J.F. Sellés, *Conocer y amar*, cap. I, ep. 4: Diferencia intencional.

From this perspective, the "nationalist-socialist" interpretation of Nietzsche is of less significance, although its practical consequences and its outcome are devastating. The absurdity of unbridled destructive power, which chills secularized hope, seems to have been unleashed. For example, the Marxist hope of overcoming the division of labor—Marx's multipurpose man—is incapable of prevailing over the concentration of the will's power in destruction. Suddenly we have found that secularized hopes are futile in the face of the coming about of nothingness. We must not maintain the disconnected hopes that hide the same incapacity to love; they are ways of going back to masking oneself: like a strategy of dissimulation.

For its part, anthropological nihilism reveals itself as the theft of the will whose productive nature is, in turn, the destruction of love. This theft is not that of Prometheus. First, because Prometheus did not steal the will from the gods, but rather the divine spark without which man cannot live: intelligence. Second, because the Promethean theft does not imply the generosity of the divine will; it tries, instead, to supplant it. The theft of the will involves the Revelation of love. And that is what is terrible. Nietzsche is nevertheless quite theatrical. His metaphysics of the artist is exercised as the will of a writer.

3.8 The hopeful task

We can simplify the question by returning to what was said concerning hope as a task. The task is one of the dimensions of hope inasmuch as hope is the unfolding of the person's gifting capacity. Consequently, the entire "structure" of hope is obtained not from the analysis of the notion, but from its integration in man, that is, by attending to the human dimensions that come together in existing according to hope.

From this perspective, the elements of hope are the following: the subject who carries out the task; the resources need to carry it out; the risk or factors of uncertainty—the adverse—and the beneficiary or recipient. But the decisive element still needs to be added, and that is the one who entrusts the task, from whom the most important help will come. Briefly: the complete structure of human hope consists of persons, task, resources, risk (or adversaries), beneficiary and the one who assigns the task (from whom the greatest help comes). Existence completely lived in hope implies all these elements.

Hope, of course, implies a subject: without it, the task is impossible, and hope would be a utopia. Since hope is in the order of love, it requires a beneficiary or recipient, which must be other than the subject. Risks appear in the task because the resources are not all there—this is what Nietzsche does not accept—, and also because there is always an adversary. But it is also necessary that the task be well directed, that is, ultimately, that there be a response. Someone has entrusted it to me: the task is not mine only from myself, because I am a person as a relationship in the origin.

It is clear that the theft of the will that Nietzsche carries out ignores this last element, since this theft is done in favor of the I (which is useless if I am person). It is from the one who entrusts me with the task that the greatest help for complementing my contribution comes; that is, that which will ensure that the risk that I am taking does not end in catastrophe. Before convoking other collaborators, I am myself a collaborator of the one who entrusts me with the task.

In any case, if any of these elements is disregarded, hope is incomplete in its structure. Modern nihilism follows from the restriction of elements to which the hopeful task has been subjected by ideologies. Such ideologies are cultural constraints within Christianity's sphere of historical influence. There are partial cultural Christians who lack faith. The Church should not be confused with the twists and turns of cultural currents influenced by Christianity.

Without the totality of its elements, human hope breaks down and gives way to utopia. This happens both to the liberal individualist as well as to the collectivist[91]. In Marx the invisible hand is the dialectical process whose subject is impersonal. The adversary is class struggle, and the beneficiary is a future society that Marx defines only negatively. Thus, the tragic in modern anthropology is an abandoned, residual, and random hope.

In this sense, for example, a partial cultural Christian can be an individualist—the pagan is not an individualist, as Hegel notes—. What does the individualist say about hope? He maintains, of course, that I am the subject of the task. What does the task consist of? Of the will to power or, more modestly, of success (even though the notion of success is rather confused). And the beneficiary? The individualist says: me. Here we have a serious constraint. Resources? Nothing but my own. Adversaries? The individualist says: everyone else. Who assigns the task? Answer: no one. The individualist is a peninsular being, surrounded on all sides by no one but one being: himself. This is nihilism.

3.9 Business and hope

So, could this be the image of a businessman? Can a businessman be like this? No. A businessman is a man who exists in hope. More precisely, he is a businessman to the extent that he accepts all the elements that make the business a task. Otherwise he is a pure speculator or an old-fashioned capitalist. Can a businessman be an individualist? What if he is? This has already been pointed out: his will opens up to nothingness. By what is a business started? By one's own will. But the will is nihilistic if it does not seek agreement with the will of the others, above all with the absolutely holy will.

Whoever declares himself an atheist and undertakes something, does not act as a person. If a personal God does not exist, then man is not a person. If no one made me, then no one has given me a task. If there is no room for this en-

---

[91] See L. Polo, "La empresa frente al socialismo y el liberalismo" (*Obras completas de Leonardo Polo*, v. XXV, Eunsa, Pamplona 2015, pp. 279-302).

dorsement of my performance, then I do not know what I am ultimately bound by, since I lack the indispensable critical criterion: to whose call do I respond?

On the other hand, a business without benefits is absurd. But who is the beneficiary of a business? Does the businessman convoke or contract external hires? How is that different from pagan slavery? And the resources? One's own cunning, one's own calculation. Who do I trust? No one: the others are hired workers, competitors, and the State, which is interventionist.

For this reason, whoever approaches his task in this way finds himself surrounded by nothingness, like Nietzsche. The businessman's task, which is beneficial and fruitful, finds itself caught up in a crisis of the structure of hope that stifles it. Adam Smith's view has already been commented upon elsewhere: the economy is a zero-sum social game saved by the "invisible hand"[92]. The invisible hand is the recourse to utopia, not the help that is integrated into the task, but rather an impersonal providence, a natural law. To unmask this is to find, as Nietzsche does, nothingness. For Nietzsche too, life is purely business: making the superman. What is the real reason behind this business? Nietzsche admits it: man cannot make God. Productively, man is compelled to atheism. Nietzsche is ignorant of God's intimacy because he reduces the I to a situation of destitution. He does not know himself to be convoked. But, in the end, he knows that the will to power is transcended.

In sum, the man who takes up the great possibilities of the Christian tradition embarks upon a hope-filled task. The integrity of hope rests on divine initiative, for hope is the initiative of the person that I am, not of a blind will. And I am a person because God is.

---

[92] See *¿Quién es el hombre?*, cap. V: La economía: 1. Los intercambios y la ciencia económica (*Obras completas de Leonardo Polo*, v. X, Eunsa, Pamplona 2016, pp. 81-82).

On the other hand, education is also a business as long as it is a hope-filled task[93]. The starting point, the central conviction required of an educator, is that she in fact conceives her activity as a way of promoting: as the work of fostering human dignity[94]. For this reason, I consider the pedagogy of self-pity, of self-commiseration to be mistaken. Hope is extremely important in education. And since the businessman lives hope (even though at present it is carried out in an unbridled manner), in this sense the businessman's job is very similar to education. If education were to be firmly taken up, then certain gaps would vanish like fog vanishes with the sun in the morning.

Obviously, man cannot work without knowing. But it is also clear that in order for one be able to devote oneself to the cultivation of knowledge, a certain instrumental sufficiency is required, since the possibilities of exercising contemplative operations in a situation of pure survival are scarce.

Slavery is not a very widespread phenomenon in Greek history; it depends on the period. Nevertheless, the spread of slavery meant a social crisis for Greece, and this was so for one fundamental reason: because Attica and the Peloponnese are territories of low agricultural productivity. The increase in the number of slaves, which was a consequence of wars, led to the collapse of Greek life. The Athenian maritime empire expanded slavery; but the defeat of Athens in the Peloponnesian War made the situation untenable. Certainly, if economic activities are put in the hands of slaves, the citizen can be largely free of them. Citizens can then devote a part of their activity to dialogue and to the cultivation of knowledge. But that does not always happen. This is the problem of free time, about

---

[93] On this topic, see L. Polo, *Ayudar a crecer. Cuestiones filosóficas de la educación* (*Obras completas de Leonardo Polo*, v. XVIII, Eunsa, Pamplona 2019, pp. 141-308). Also see: F. Altarejos, "Finalidad y libertad en educación", *Anuario Filosófico*, XXIX/2 (1996), 333-345; E. R. Moros – J. M. Izaguirre, *La acción educativa según la antropología trascendental de Leonardo Polo*, Cuadernos de Anuario Filosófico, Serie Universitaria, n° 197, Servicio de Publicaciones de la Universidad de Navarra, Pamplona 2007.

[94] See J. M. Izaguirre – R. Moros, "La tarea del educador: la sindéresis", *Studia Poliana*, 9 (2007), 103-127.

which we have already spoken. In the Roman Empire slavery is a central fact, but slavery also destroyed the Roman Empire.

The family is the basic social institution[95]. Consequently, it is also a plexus that is subject to description. For example, on weekends many elderly people fall ill in Madrid. Something very unusual. What makes this epidemic possible? We all know what is happening: on the weekends the family takes the car and goes to the Sierra. The elderly person is a nuisance, and he has to be brought to the hospital. It is the exclusion of the elderly from the family plexus.

What is the relationship between generations? Marriage is a mutual gift that has a purpose. To reduce it to a corporeal exchange is to separate what is medial in marriage from its natural end, which is generation. This destroys the family. Thus, the family is also a business since it has a common objective, which are the children: their procreation and their education[96]. To carry a child forward from her birth until she is ready (shall we say) to become independent, is a task that takes years. Another example: the world of a fetus is the maternal womb. What is abortion? The expulsion of a man from his world[97].

---

[95] See Polo, "Projecto sobre la familia" (*Obras completas de Leonardo Polo*, v. XXIII, Eunsa, Pamplona 2012, pp. 25-53).

[96] See L. Polo, "El hombre como hijo" (*Obras completas de Leonardo Polo*, v. XVI, Eunsa, Pamplona 2018, pp. 157-165).

[97] Polo points out that it is killing a project. See *Comentarios a la "Mulieris dignitatem"*, pro manuscripto.

Books by Leonardo Polo

Complete works in Spanish

Obras Completas de Leonardo Polo, Serie A, Vol. I-XXVII, Eunsa, Pamplona 2015-2019

Obras Completas de Leonardo Polo, Serie B: Inéditos, Vol. XVIII- , Eunsa, Pamplona 2020-present

English Translations of Polo's Works

1. *Ethics. A Modern Version of Its Classic Themes.* (Sinag-Tala Publishers, Manila 2008)
2. *Why a Transcendental Anthropology?* (Leonardo Polo Institute of Philosophy Press, South Bend 2014)
3. "Human Feelings" in the *Journal of Polian Studies* (2014)
4. "Friendship in Aristotle" in the *Journal of Polian Studies* (2015)
5. "University Professor" in *The European Conservative* (Winter/Spring 2016)
6. "On the Origin of Man: Hominization and Humanization" in the *Journal of Polian Studies* (2016)
7. *Rich and Poor* (Leonardo Polo Institute of Philosophy Press, South Bend 2017)
8. "Being and Communication" in the *Journal of Polian Studies* (2017)
9. "Lo radical y la Libertad" in *Freedom in Quarantine* by Daniel Bernardus (2020)
10. "Hope" in the *Journal of Polian Studies* (2022)